RUCKING
& ROLLING

RUCKING & ROLLING

60 YEARS OF INTERNATIONAL RUGBY

PETER BILLS

796/333

FOREWORD BY **GEORGE HOOK**

FEATURING EXCLUSIVE CONTRIBUTIONS FROM:
SIR ANTHONY O'REILLY, COLIN MEADS,
GARETH EDWARDS, JEAN-PIERRE RIVES,
DAVID CAMPESE & MARTIN JOHNSON

MERCIER PRESS
WHAT YOU NEED TO READ

This book is dedicated to the memory of Lang Jones, a great man who loved and served the sport of rugby football all his life. A teacher at King Edward's School, Bath for 40 years, he was known by countless numbers in West Country rugby, including international players and ordinary schoolboys who played the game under his tutelage. He will be sorely missed.

Lang Jones 1936–2007

MERCIER PRESS
Douglas Village, Cork
www.mercierpress.ie

Trade enquiries to CMD Distribution
55A Spruce Avenue, Stillorgan Industrial Park,
Blackrock, County Dublin

ISBN: 978-1-85635-557-5

10 9 8 7 6 5 4 3 2 1

A CIP record for this title is available from the British Library

 Mercier Press receives financial assistance from the Arts
Council/An Chomhairle Ealaíon

Project Art Editor: Luke Griffin
Designer: David Etherington
Picture Research: Paul Langan
Production: Peter Hinton
Editorial: Jo Murray

Printed in Dubai

Several people helped me with this book. I would like to thank my
agent John Pawsey, who made the connections and the design and
editorial team at Carlton Books, who worked with flair and passion to
ensure the book crossed the try line.

And also thanks to my family – Averil, Hannah, Katie and James
who put up with a good deal of inattention while I worked on the
publication.

This does not pretend to be *the* quintessential record of the last sixty
years of international rugby. What it does seek to portray are the ebbs
and flows of the rugby tide, a sea that is forever moving and changing.

Previous page:
Former All Black captain
and fan favourite Wayne
'Buck' Shelford.

Contents

Foreword BY GEORGE HOOK

The professional game has taken such a hold on the psyche of the modern rugby supporter that there is increasingly a sense that it was always thus. Yet in a decade and a half the game will celebrate the 200th anniversary of William Webb Ellis's innovation that founded the game. On that anniversary, the players will have been playing for pay for little over ten per cent of the life of the game.

Peter Bills has done the game a service by charting the history of the modern game over the last 50 or more years. He has straddled the difficult divide of writing a history full of scholarship that remains entertaining and certainly will not fill the dusty shelves of academic libraries.

By interviewing true rugby men of strong opinions like Tony O'Reilly, Colin Meads and David Campese, he has given the story an authority born of true experience. Listening to Meads through Peter's prose gives a clear indication of a hard man who was willing to admit that his game suffered when he was made captain.

O'Reilly bemoans the dreadful officiating of local referees during the Lions tour in 1959 to New Zealand. Readers will probably smile as they read Mead's self-same complaint about South Africa when his own country had benefited so often when playing at home. What shines through these interviews is the wonderful spirit those tours engendered in players from all countries who toured abroad. O'Reilly and Meads are as one on the value of the game.

The strength of this book is that Peter Bills has succeeded, probably because of his own standing in the game, to elicit strong views from players. Nowhere is that better exemplified than in the analysis of the professional game by David Campese and François Pienaar. Campese, despite a reputation as a money earner in the quasi-amateur days of the game, still believes that part-time professionals might have learned more about life. Pienaar pointedly reminds us of the shambles that was the rush towards the professional game.

For Irish readers, this book will bring unhappy memories of trips to Cardiff against the great Wales side of the 1970s and happier thoughts about the involvement of Irish players on the same ground in the greatest rugby match ever played, when the Barbarians beat the mighty All Blacks. Great Irish players and moments litter a text that is both a prodder of memory and a reminder of joyous times.

The growth in the popularity of rugby has meant that there has been a similar explosion in the number of books about the sport. Sadly few have lived up to the story they attempted to tell. The last fifty years have been a roller-coaster ride for everybody involved in the game and any telling of that period needs to be written in a style that captures the changes in law, attitudes and ultimately remuneration. Peter Bills has done the game and its players proud in a work that zips along at the same pace as a game played on a firm sod in Paris under blue skies in the spring.

George Hook
Dublin, 2007

Introduction

'Detested sport that owes its pleasures to another's pain' wrote the English essayist William Cowper in the 18th century.

Well yes, but who wouldn't accept a bit of pain for all the glory, the rip-roaring fun and vibrancy of rugby football?

For sure, the last sixty years of this game in an international sense have been the most fantastic, the most exciting and by far the most dramatic in the entire history of the sport. Rugby football in those years has mirrored perfectly 20th-century life: it has opened up, the blinkers have been removed and cast aside.

We've seen dramatic events, great players, fearsome confrontations and acts and deeds that have brought a warm glow to the soul. Like the joyous celebrations of the liberated South African President Nelson Mandela upon seeing the Springbok captain François Pienaar lift the 1995 Rugby World Cup for his country in Johannesburg. Has any image in the history of the sport so epitomized what rugby union can do, how it can bring people together, provide unity, cohesion and hope where hitherto there was division and doubt?

The last sixty years of rugby football have provided a kaleidoscope of colour, noise and excitement both on and off the playing fields of the world. The coming of the Rugby World Cup signalled the sport's move to a professional code; its old amateur roots were worthy and wondrous, but ultimately untenable in the modern world. To expect young men to give up their time for nothing except the pleasure of the game was a Victorian concept: meritorious and splendid in its day, but with a distinct shelf-life. But the irony was, it was eventually proved flawed and undermined by the authorities, those so-called 'guardians' of the amateur ethos, who welcomed into the game sponsors with deep pockets filled with cash. That broke up completely the amateur concept.

This is a sport that has evolved. In the 1950s, as you can read in the pages of this book, fun and frivolity were at the core of the game. Most played it simply as an excuse for the wonderful social life it offered and even those at the highest levels could never be accused of taking it that seriously.

But in some countries of the world, it was a great deal more than a vehicle for laughs. Attitudes in the tough southern hemisphere lands of New Zealand and South Africa were vastly different and those views would ultimately prevail upon the whole world, forcing the countries of the northern hemisphere to adopt a more pragmatic approach.

Through the last sixty years, rugby has rucked and rolled its way into the headlines of the international media. It has lured royalty, presidents and prime ministers to its great occasions and, on a more humble level, has been a forum for bringing people together. All over the world, people associated with this great game continue to do marvellous deeds on its behalf. Young men tragically injured or crippled by accidents on the playing field find friends they never knew existed, as people offer

Opposite: Wales international Keith Jarrett lines up a goal kick at the London Welsh ground.

generous financial help or give practical assistance. The term 'rugby's family' is one widely used but it is no mere expression; rather, a vibrant, ever eager association offering great bonhomie, kindness and help to anyone requiring it.

On the field these past sixty years, there have been some momentous times. If one had to pick a fantasy team of the world's greatest, perhaps it would be right and proper to focus on the wonderful forwards produced by New Zealand in the 1960s and the great three-quarters who, albeit briefly, put British and Irish rugby on top of the world in the first half of the 1970s.

Becoming an All Black has always been the greatest desire of every living male New Zealander. Typically, All Blacks are renowned as strong, powerful forwards with great presence and ball skills. Of course, down the years there have been myriad examples of this particular species but the 1960s seemed to bring together a unique collection of such men. The likes of Wilson Whineray, Colin Meads, Kel Tremain, Brian Lochore, Ken Gray and Waka Nathan were peerless in their class. They helped make New Zealand the greatest rugby nation on earth in their era.

Then, out of the ashes of three losing Lions tours in the 1960s came a squad of British and Irish players who took the world game onto a new, exciting plateau. This was masterminded by a crop of brilliant young Welshmen exuding class and skill: Gareth Edwards, Barry John, Gerald Davies, J. P. R. Williams, Phil Bennett, John Dawes and J. J. Williams. And that was just the backs. When you added on forwards such as Mervyn Davies, John Taylor, Graham Price and his mates in the Pontypool front row it was little wonder that Wales ruled northern hemisphere rugby throughout the decade of the 1970s.

And to strengthen the British and Irish Lions for their historic 1971 tour when they became the first (and still the only) Lions touring party in history to win a Test series in New Zealand, there were the likes of Mike Gibson, Ray McLoughlin, Willie John McBride, Fergus Slattery, Gordon Brown and David Duckham. Never has the sun shone so brilliantly upon British and Irish rugby.

But who can ignore the talents of so many gifted players in two other major rugby-playing lands of the world, South Africa and France? The story of South Africa's evolution over the last sixty years is, for the most part, a painful one. The poisonous apartheid system that, in the end, turned South African against South African had sour repercussions for the sport in the country. Because of it, the Springbok emblem became a pariah in the world game, rejected by all decent and fair-minded people who were revolted by the political system existing in the country under a dictatorial white regime. It couldn't last and it didn't, but it is still appropriate to enquire of certain international rugby countries and individual players, whether by continuing to send touring parties to that country, they prolonged the agony of apartheid and shored up the blinkered regime in South Africa.

Any activity worthy of its name inevitably strays into the choppy waters of politics, and rugby has been no exception. But South Africa's re-emergence as a genuine democratic nation following Mandela's release and the free elections of the early 1990s meant that bitter divisions could be put aside. Most marvellously of all, a new Springbok era dawned, with talented young black players such as Ashwin Willemse

Australia's players can only watch as England's fly-half Jonny Wilkinson drops the goal that dramatically wins the 2003 World Cup in Sydney.

and Bryan Habana earning by right the coveted Springbok jersey. These and so many young men like them have been and continue to be outstanding ambassadors not just for their newly unified nation but the sport in general. Rugby union has been a better game for their presence.

The same can be said of Australia, so far the only country to have won the World Cup twice. Given that at the start of the period which this book covers, the 1950s, and for many years thereafter, rugby union in the country was regarded as an also-ran against the omnipresent rugby league, the progress of the sport in that land has been nothing less than sensational. Great men have performed stirring deeds on behalf of the game in Australia; the likes of Bob Dwyer, Bob Templeton, Nick Shehadie, Alan Jones, the Ella brothers, Andrew Slack, Michael Lynagh, David Campese, John Eales, Simon Poidevin, Michael Foley, Tim Horan and a whole cluster more. The traditionally competitive Australians have not only produced a whole glut of fine sides but also staged the greatest Rugby World Cup to date, in 2003.

As for the French, so many gloriously talented, unpredictable players have strutted the stage, as proud as cockerels ruffling their feathers. There have been fine, fast, ball-handling forwards and wondrous backs blessed with silky skills and talents honed from youth by the mighty clubs of the country.

France has provided what we might term the wine and the elegance to rugby's staple dish. Without them, the game worldwide would have been so much poorer. And now, eagerly thrusting their noses around the door marked 'world rugby' for a glimpse of life in this hallowed club, come countries like Italy, Argentina, Japan and the Pacific Islands. But therein lies the next challenge for the game, the urgent need to offer more opportunities and closer integration to these ambitious countries.

But that is for the future. For the present, let us recall with pleasure the progress of this sport over the last sixty years, living briefly through these pages some of the great deeds that have captured the imagination of so many in that time.

Peter Bills, 2007

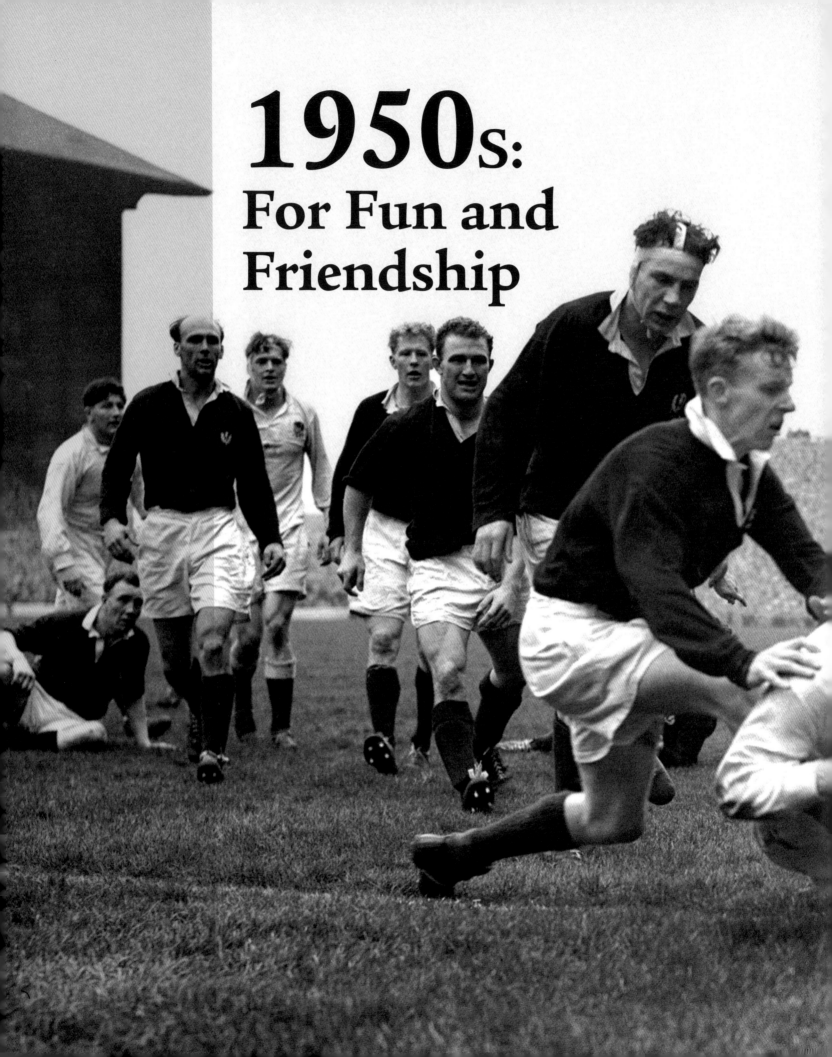

1950s:
For Fun and Friendship

1950s: For Fun and Friendship

Post-war rugby was a game divided. For the purposes of simplicity, it is convenient to use the equator as the defining line. Above it, it was seen as a game, and little more. Below it, by contrast, rugby represented a bold and serious assertion of nationhood.

In countries like England, Ireland and Scotland, bastions of the great amateur ethos, it was regarded as little more than a social pastime, a sporting activity bred, in the main, by the private schools. In Wales, the grammar schools produced a stream of skilled, talented players but the tough inner core came from the forwards, products of the great mines and steelworks that were so emblematic a part of the Welsh landscape.

There were no leagues in those times. What made matches in northern hemisphere countries like Wales and France ultra-competitive, was local pride. Thus, games like Cardiff v Newport and, in France, Lourdes v Tarbes, were fiercely combative affairs. Punches frequently flew, accepted as a regular and common occurrence in those particular countries but abhorred by the powers that be in countries like England.

By complete and glorious contrast, there existed in England a devotion to the amateur concept. Training was frowned upon, coaches were unheard of and players never saw rugby as anything much more than a pleasing diversion. They played largely for fun, for friendship, for frivolity. Their incentive was solely the honour of representing their club or country. Any associated glory that might rub off was greeted with self-effacing good humour. After all, they were chaps there just to have fun with their pals.

Then, on Monday mornings, whether they had played for a veteran's team, Harlequins or England, they would still take the train or tube among the bowler-hat brigade heading for work in the City of London. The supporters were much the same. The game was viewed almost as something of a quaint distraction, followed by a minority of the population (attendances at most club matches were modest), a world apart from the hordes who watched professional football.

Club players who wished to go skiing during the northern winter, would simply book up and go. The club just wouldn't see them for a couple of weeks. As one London Irish player said, 'You never knew who was playing until you saw the team sheet up on the wall. Then you'd say, "Gee, look who's in our team this week".'

In all spheres, attitudes were extraordinary. In the early 1950s, Robin Thompson, later to be selected as captain of the 1955 Lions in South Africa, was chosen for his international debut for Ireland. Thompson, an analytical

> 'You never knew who was playing until you saw the team sheet up on the wall. Then you'd say, "Gee, look who's in our team this week".'

Previous pages: England's Peter Thompson dives over to score his team's second try against Scotland in 1957. England won 16-3.

Opposite: British & Irish Lions captain Robin Thompson warms up during a training session, shortly before the squad's departure for the 1955 tour of South Africa.

chemist, was working for Glaxo in London and sought out his boss to ask if he might have the following Friday off, 'to go and play for Ireland'.

He was told curtly, 'No, you may not. Go back to your bench. It is not even for England.'

Thompson informed the Irish Rugby Football Union he would not be allowed to meet up the day prior to the match. But strings were pulled, and his release was eventually sanctioned. Yet this spoke volumes about the limited value of even international rugby in the northern hemisphere at that time.

A great dichotomy existed in standards and attitudes between the two hemispheres. Countries of the southern hemisphere like New Zealand and South Africa saw their international rugby team as a worldwide advertisement for their land, one of the driving forces of promotion for the entire country. This was no simple game, something to be taken lightly. The badge of the All Blacks, the famous silver fern, and the dashing, leaping springbok that denoted South Africa, represented statehood.

Australia was by no means the force it was to become, yet here, too, chests swelled with pride when the national jersey was worn. And, as ever with Australians, sport was a highly competitive activity, to be taken seriously. This difference in philosophies was at the root of southern hemisphere hegemony for so many years.

Rugby football of that era was a very different beast to contemporary times. To play with your friends, to tour a faraway country in the southern hemisphere for anything up to six months at a time, was considered the zenith of these young men's ambitions. Sport, just about any sport, still enjoyed the halcyon days of pleasure and pride: certainly in sports that were strictly amateur, the ogre of money was never mentioned. This however, was about to change.

> 'No, you may not. Go back to your bench. It is not even for England.'

Money: The Great Unmentionable

In 1955, the young rugby men of Great Britain and Ireland had been astonished to arrive for the first Test match against South Africa in Johannesburg and witness a vast crowd estimated at as many as 104,000 people. Whatever the precise figure, none of these young rugby tourists had ever seen anything like it. The finances involved for those times were simply staggering, much in excess of anything envisaged in the northern hemisphere.

Then, in 1959, on the British & Irish Lions tour of New Zealand, interest was such that very nearly 800,000 people paid to go and see the tourists, led by Irishman Ronnie Dawson, at their 25 matches on the north and south islands. Remarkably, this represented, at that time, almost half the entire population of that country nestling down in the icy waters, not a thousand miles from the Antarctic wastes.

Opposite: England's Peter Jackson is about to kick to touch against Australia at Twickenham in 1958. England won the close game 9–6.

Wales's Jack Matthews touches down for a try against France in the 1950 Grand Slam win.

Between them, they spent something in the region of £300,000 in tickets to see those Lions, an extraordinary sum of money for those days. Yet the rugby players they had come to see, many of whom had made their reputation four years earlier with the Lions in South Africa, received expenses of just £2 a week: a pittance, an absurdity. Frankly, it represented ridiculous parsimony. Indeed, some had had to put their careers on hold back home, and travelled without any sort of payment whatever from their posts.

The imbalance between around 100,000 people paying good money at the gate to watch players at a single game, in an amateur sport, whilst those players received not a penny for the demonstration of their skills and efforts, not to mention the sacrifices they made in terms of their time and careers, cannot escape the modern-day observer. But in those times, financial gain was never courted, never allowed to stain the name of a game whose very struts were the strict amateur code. Only in France was reality embraced.

But in Britain and Ireland it was considered that those who did wish to pursue money, a vulgar exercise in the eyes of the crusty colonels, madcap majors and those gentlemen who administered rugby union, could join one of the rugby league clubs in the North of England where payment was permitted. Alas, should a player decide to do so, he would render a priest's excommunication something of a slap on the wrist by comparison, so total was the revulsion on the part of those he left behind.

Rugby union accepted with a traditional stiff upper lip the loss of some outstanding talents to the professional code. Lewis Jones, the outstanding Welsh wing, departed in 1952; a few years later, England's fine centre Jeff Butterfield was approached by two men in a wood, whilst out for a training run one day. Introducing themselves without ceremony as the sweating, panting Butterfield looked on bemused, they promptly opened a suitcase they carried with them containing, they assured their target, £6,000 in cash. In those days, that would have been enough for the highly talented, respected English centre to buy a few streets full of houses and a Rolls-Royce. Butterfield smiled and resumed his run.

   Nobody could see in those days that there lay at the heart of this great sport, a gross discrepancy, a lie if you like. That lie was buried for decades, the reality ignored, hushed up or rendered irrelevant by the times in which people lived. Thus, the young men making their way into rugby union's dressing rooms and bars of that time, did so for the sheer *joie de vivre*, the fun and love of it all. They carried with them a whiff of the spirit of an earlier generation, young men who had cheerfully sacrificed themselves for the cause of their country. This was different; rugby, after all, was only a game. But the same attitudes prevailed, the same sense of serving the cause, especially at international level. Yet while they played for the fun, the glory and the honour, the unions were quietly making a handsome return from their talents.

England's Jeff Butterfield leads the team out under the watchful eye of the police.

The Lions in South Africa

Those two tours undertaken by the Lions in 1955 and 1959 epitomized the age, the era. Truly, these were rugby union's halcyon days. Arguably, the vintage of 1955 was the best of the two and perhaps the finest Lions ever, matched in class and quality only by the 1971 tourists. They went to a land where men of white Afrikaner background grew huge, their muscles honed by work on the ubiquitous, white-owned farms.

Rugby football was, by a distance, the preferred sporting pastime of these South African people and they revelled in the physicality of the contest.

In 1955, when the Lions selectors sat down to dinner and the task of choosing the thirty players for the tour, they had a delicate assignment. The sensation of the recently concluded Five Nations Championship season was a young Irishman of striking looks, biting humour and intense intellect more befitting a man of many years, than a youngster.

Anthony Joseph Francis O'Reilly possessed a mercurial talent, and he was also immensely gifted as a sportsman. He played rugby, ran the 100 and 200 metres in athletics, excelled at cricket and was a fine tennis player. Yet the man chosen as Lions captain that year, Robin Thompson of Northern Ireland, had warned the selectors prior to their meeting: 'Don't choose O'Reilly; don't spoil him for the future by bringing him on too early. His time will come but this tour is too soon for him. He is too young.'

Thompson was a highly intelligent man but a lousy judge of rugby players. Tony O'Reilly went on the tour, scored twenty tries in twenty-one matches and established a reputation that would be remembered sixty years later. He became, literally, one of rugby's first star players.

O'Reilly impressed everyone with whom he came into contact with his gregarious nature, his confidence, wit and sharp brain. It is the preserve of few young men to enjoy such qualities at 18 years of age. But as the Welsh fly-half of that tour, Cliff Morgan, said memorably, 'At just 18, Tony was the youngest player of all, but he was more like a man of 30, and probably the most intelligent of all.'

The young Irishman possessed a sense of humour every bit as delicious as a fine South African wine. No sooner had those 1955 tourists arrived in the country at Johannesburg airport – the first Lions ever to fly to the southern hemisphere incidentally, albeit via just about every city between London and Johannesburg – than they were taken to watch a provincial match not far from their (then) Transvaal base.

O'Reilly took a look for a short time, mused carefully at what was going on in front of him and turned to a friend and playing colleague beside him. 'Isn't that the biggest, meanest pack of forwards you have ever seen on a rugby field?' he enquired. 'And isn't that ground the hardest you've ever seen in your life to fall on? And isn't there a flight to London from Johannesburg tonight and shouldn't we be on it?'

And so it began, a long, enervating twenty-five-match tour spanning around sixteen weeks. They left London on 16 June and arrived home on the last day of September. They saw sights, sounds and situations beyond the imagination of young men who, in some cases, had hitherto travelled no further than the borders of the British Isles and Ireland.

'South Africa', as someone once noted, 'was renowned both far and wide for politics and little else beside.' The Lions found a whole lot more, however.

Sexual attitudes in countries like Ireland and England in that era, were conventional, to say the least. But what the Lions found when they got to South Africa was a very different scenario. Lions captain Robin Thompson said in 2002 before his death: 'The New Zealand All Blacks had been there in 1949 and afterwards, eight girls whom they had met became pregnant. This was a scandal at the time. But when we got there in 1955, it quickly became clear that you could have slept with a married or single woman every night of the tour, if you'd wanted to. The women just threw themselves at you everywhere you went. The girls were from really well-to-do families. Some of them travelled all around the country, just following the Lions. They were educated, monied women; it was astonishing. Today, they would be called groupies.

'It was a real eye-opener at that time because remember, we had come from Britain and Ireland in the mid-1950s when getting your hands on a girl's breasts was an achievement. So it shocked everybody in the party how amoral sexually South Africa was. It was one of the most amazing things at that time bearing in mind the innate conservatism of the country. But we quickly came to realize it was a false conservatism. Most of the women out there had servants and nothing else to do.'

In fact, the ultra-conservative Lions management was so concerned that when they heard one player was involved with a woman, the manager is alleged to have threatened to write to the player's parish priest.

As for the rugby, a dramatic first Test at Johannesburg's famous Ellis Park lured around 100,000 South Africans to witness what came to be known as one of the most famous games in the long history of the sport. It was decided in the Lions favour, 23 points to 22, only because the South African full-back Jack van der Schyff missed a last-minute conversion that would have won the game.

South Africans took the sport deadly seriously; this was no pastime for fun, friendship and relaxation. In their eyes South Africa was the most powerful rugby nation on earth, had never (at that time) lost a Test series to the feared New Zealanders and an opening Test defeat by the Lions went down as badly as a tumbling gold price on the high veld. The South African prime minister went into the Lions dressing room after the game to announce: 'Well done, but this is a terrible day for South Africa'. The Lions players thought he was joking; alas,

'Isn't that the biggest, meanest pack of forwards you have ever seen on a rugby field? And isn't that ground the hardest you've ever seen in your life to fall on? And isn't there a flight to London ... And shouldn't we be on it?'

Following pages: British & Irish Lion Billy Williams is pursued by the Springbok forward Salty Du Rand as he kicks the ball up-field. South Africa won this fourth Test played at Port Elizabeth 22–8.

he was deadly serious. The next day, one of the local newspapers had a cartoon drawing of the Prime Minister and the South African rugby selectors walking up the plank onto a ship named *Abroad*. It was taken that seriously.

This was the contrast between attitudes in the northern and southern hemispheres. The Springboks played to win; nothing else mattered. Their supporters demanded victory as an extension of their imagined supremacy as a people. Losing to anyone could not be tolerated.

Thus, whilst the Lions played schoolboy jokes on each other, furtively (in the case of the late Clem Thomas) collected, stored and then sold for profit the packets of cigarettes handed to players as gifts, and enjoyed themselves in the most self-indulgent of activities, the South Africans were addressing the ramifications of that first Test defeat as though it were an early battle in a war. For them it was.

They trained assiduously, prepared extensively and adopted an approach that was akin to professionalism. It paid off in the form of a 25-9 victory in the second Test at Cape Town, but was again found wanting as the Lions took a tightly contested third Test, 9-6, at Pretoria, a city at the very heart of Afrikanerdom. The locals were beside themselves with despair and anger.

> 'It quickly became clear that you could have slept with a married or single woman every night of the tour, if you'd wanted to.'

Take the message the 1955 South African team captain, Stephen Fry, received from one irate supporter following the Springboks' third Test defeat at Pretoria. 'Dear Mr Fry,' it read, 'It is high time that you opened your eyes and realized that as far as football is concerned, you are a failure. The sooner you say farewell to the game and withdraw entirely from the team, the better it will be for your health.

'If you ignore this warning it will be too late for sorrow. You have very likely received several similar letters. The only difference between those and this one is that if you ignore it you will not have the pleasure of leaving the field as Stephen Fry. Indeed, the title "late" will appear before your name. Even if I have to pay for it with my own life I will do so willingly, for I will know that I have done so in the interests of our national game.'

By wonderful contrast with all this intensity, a couple of the Lions players devised cunning ploys to find the best parties in town on their tour and get themselves invited on a Saturday evening after the match. 'We used to drive up to Jan Smuts Avenue, one of the smartest areas of Johannesburg, in a car someone had lent us for the evening,' recalled Irish three-quarter Cecil Pedlow. 'We'd see a lot of cars parked outside a house, see all the lights on and knock on the door.

'We'd say something like, "Oh, do you know where so and so road is", or "do you know where the Van Rensburgs live?" Of course, they were all hypothetical. But we'd be wearing our Lions blazers and ties and suddenly, there'd be a shout from the guy at the front door – "Hey, it's Tony O'Reilly and his pal from the Lions at the door."

'Of course, we'd be invited in, entertained regally and have a wonderful time. It always worked.'

The scowling, snarling, sweating Springboks were enduring a rather less riotous preparation for their last meeting with the tourists. They simply had to triumph in the final Test at Port Elizabeth and against a tired, injury-ravaged and, in some cases, homesick Lions team, they did, 22-8. It tied the series at 2-2 but few could escape the conclusion that the Lions had, over the course of their twenty-five games (nineteen of which were won) provided rugby of a supreme quality and attraction. The darting, fleet-footed backs, players like O'Reilly, Morgan and the English centre Jeff Butterfield, one of the finest passers of a ball the game had known, had exposed many leaden-footed opponents. These Lions had possessed not just quality but class, on and off the field.

And they had fun. As Cliff Morgan said some time later, 'It was an adventure. It wasn't all about winning matches, about tactics, about watching endless videotapes. It was fun.'

Bryn Meredith and Rees Williams of the Lions rush to block a kick from the Springbok scrum-half Tommy Gentles during the first Test at Ellis Park, Johannesburg in 1955. The Lions won 23-22.

The International Rugby Grounds

International grounds of yesteryear were rudimentary affairs. Splinters in the backside and aching muscles were all part of the day out, and that was for the so-called lucky ones who had seats.

Few of the old grounds had many comforts. They were unrecognizable to the swank, modern stadiums of contemporary times.

Cardiff Arms Park was another place of strictly limited facilities, for players and spectators. Those attending matches readied themselves to be crammed in on international match days, but as for the atmosphere; well, it was raw-boned and unique. They poured out of the city pubs just across the street from the stadium to roar their support for their beloved Wales. Curiously, the old ground doubled up as a greyhound track and those familiar lights that lit up the racing dogs provided an odd backdrop for international rugby games.

Murrayfield, where Scotland played, had vast banks of terracing and an unknown capacity. It is said that for one match against Wales in the 1960s, around 110,000 people squeezed in, thousands of them sitting on the touchline or behind the dead-ball line at each end.

Twickenham, full of those little wooden, splinter-filled seats just waiting to jag into the unwary bottom, was smaller but more intimate. Those sitting just inside the little wooden fence that ran around the ground had a wonderful insight into the game, able to hear players' calls and comments.

If, in later years, you wanted to know what these old stadiums were like, you could have visited Ireland's Lansdowne Road until the end of 2006 (when demolition and rebuilding was due to begin). There, you could see the basic accommodation, the comparative lack of hospitality space (although the west stand on the ground did contain some boxes for corporate entertainment).

In countries of the southern hemisphere, vast stands of tubular steel were erected, stretching high into the sky. Ellis Park had a towering stand that looked perilous but it offered a bird's-eye view of the game below. Great crowds of close to 100,000 could be accommodated.

Newlands Stadium, Cape Town, was built beneath the imposing Table Mountain range that dominates the Cape. Its stands were never quite as high as some built at Ellis Park, nor as perilous-looking. But if the rugby was not special to watch on a particular day, spectators could enjoy the wonderful views of the mountains at the back of the ground.

In Wellington, New Zealand, another huge stand was erected on the Athletic Park site at the southern end of the city. Those who sat in the top half of it, which was all open to the elements, would invariably be wind-lashed and feel the driving rain from one of those familiar southerly gales that batter the rugged coastline in winter.

Opposite: The old Cardiff Arms Park with the famous greyhound track around the perimeter.

Left: Twickenham Stadium is affectionately known as the 'Cabbage Patch' on account that the land where the ground stands was previously used to grow the vegetable.

Below: The original Murrayfield Stadium opened in 1925. The first visitors were England, whom Scotland beat to win their first Five Nations Championship Grand Slam.

Above: Newlands Stadium, Cape Town as it looked in the 1950s. The first international was held in 1891 when the British and Irish Lions toured South Africa.

Left: French internationals at the Colombes Stadium, Paris were renowned for being noisy, exuberant affairs. The ground was originally constructed for the 1924 Olympic Games.

British & Irish Lions captain Ronnie Dawson and All Black captain Wilson Whineray lead out their teams before the start of the first Test at Dunedin in 1959.

The Lions Return

Irishmen Tony O'Reilly and Andy Mulligan were the life and soul of the 1959 Lions tour of New Zealand. Everywhere they went, the pair made merriment. But not even they could raise a smile on the night of 18 July 1959 in the south island city of Dunedin.

That day, the Lions scored four tries to none in the first Test match against the All Blacks. Alas, New Zealand full-back Don Clarke, constantly offered opportunities by a referee who shamelessly penalized the Lions from pillar to post, booted six penalty goals to get New Zealand home 18-17.

That single Test match remains one of the most notorious in history, even nearly half a century later. New Zealand led early through Clarke's first two penalties and it took the Lions half an hour to get their first score, a penalty by Irishman David Hewitt. Just before the interval, English fly-half Bev Risman cut through the defence, sending Welsh centre Malcolm Price clear and he put Tony O'Reilly over for a thrilling try. If that was thought exciting, the Lions scored a second try before the break. Risman kicked ahead, wing Peter Jackson hacked it on and Price was up first for a second unconverted try.

The All Blacks had been stung and there was another shock for them early in the second half when Welsh lock Roddy Evans intercepted a New Zealand pass and flanker Ken Smith was up in support to send Jackson away for the Lions third try, making it 12-6.

Clarke added another goal, for yet another technical offence, this time against scrum-half Dickie Jeeps, which mystified the Lions. No matter, they got a fourth try when Risman again created the opening, Ken Scotland gathered and Price scored his second try of the game. At 17-9 for the Lions with just ten minutes left, it looked all over for the All Blacks.

But Clarke then landed two more penalties in just seven minutes, two of them awards that baffled the increasingly incensed Lions. It was 15-17 and the tension in the ground was palpable. Finally, with only two minutes left, the referee again blew his whistle, this time claiming Irish forward Gordon Wood was offside, a decision the player vigorously contested later, insisting a New Zealand player had touched the ball first.

Whatever the truth, Clarke stepped up to boot his sixth penalty of the match and put New Zealand 18-17 ahead. Even after that, the Lions looked as though they had won it. They drove play towards the New Zealand line, where lock forward Evans dashed over to touch down for what everyone thought was a fifth try and the winning score. Alas, they had reckoned without a referee who seemed to be handling a different game. He blew his whistle and penalized the Lions for 'handling in the maul'. Lions assistant manager Ossie Glasgow called the decision 'incomprehensible'. The Lions had lost 18-17 and the word 'robbed' would probably be a better description.

That esteemed New Zealand rugby writer Terry McLean called it 'the saddest victory New Zealand has ever recorded'.

Such was the crowd's ire, directed mainly at the local referee Mr A. L. Fleury, that they roared their support for the Lions for much of the second half, an extraordinary act in a country as proud of its identity as New Zealand. McLean wrote later: 'If it were possible, New Zealand would like to rub this match out of the records. Alternatively, it would pull the shades down on it and ban it as a topic of conversation in decent society.

'Mr Gordon Brown, the President of the New Zealand Rugby Union, talked bravely at the subsequent dinner of a victory which had been won "within the framework of the rules" and for which "no apologies need be offered". No doubt he was speaking his own mind. Alas, he was not speaking with the voice of New Zealand. The tremendous chants of "Red, Red, Red" which broke out as soon as New Zealand had placed the last goal, two minutes from time, expressed the resentment of the crowd of 40,000 at Carisbrook at the manner in which victory was being won. The regret which was expressed all through the tour at every little hamlet and in every big city, was a more considered but still a most telling opinion. New Zealand, it was plain, could never quite stomach such a victory.'

The Lions were so set back by that defeat they never recovered on the remainder of their tour. They lost the second Test 11-8 in Wellington, despite leading until three minutes from the end, and the third Test 22-8 in Christchurch. Not until the fourth Test in Auckland in the second half of September did they taste victory, edging out the All Blacks 9-6 at Eden Park. They out-scored the All Blacks by nine tries to seven in the Test series and played some wonderfully

> 'Within the framework of the rules ... no apologies need be offered.'

entertaining rugby. Yet the Test series was lost, chiefly due to the controversial incidents in the first Test.

Wilson Whineray, who was to win 32 caps between 1957 and 1965 and led his country supremely well, played in that series and is today regarded as New Zealand's most eminent old All Black. Now Sir Wilson, he told me at his Auckland home: 'The Lions backs on that tour were exceptional. They had so much pace, so much skill behind the scrum. But perhaps they lacked a bit of organization and what I'd call hard-core strength among the forwards. That was really where we won the series, but it was a desperately close thing. The first and second Tests went our way but we could easily have lost both.'

Whineray doffed his hat to the Lions class of 1959. But he always regarded the Springboks as New Zealand's greatest foe in those times. 'I first played against the Springboks in 1956 when they toured New Zealand. I was in the New Zealand Universities side which beat them on that trip. I remember Piet du Toit on that 1956 tour: he was a tough scrummager, technically very awkward to scrum against.'

Whineray began his Test career in 1957 and ended it after the 1965 South African tour of New Zealand. 'In 1965, I scrummaged against Andrew MacDonald, a Rhodesian farmer. He was an interesting fellow. He had about a 3,000 acre farm of mixed crops and was a hard player. But he was a nice guy, I liked him. Unfortunately, he only ever played Test rugby that single year, 1965. I don't think it was too long after when he'd got home, he got in a tangle with a lion on his land and it chewed up part of his arm. It ended his career, of course."

What made South Africa so special? 'Traditionally, they were our greatest foe. And part of the reason for that was, we didn't play them very much. When New Zealand went to South Africa for the 1960 tour, it was the first time the All Blacks had been there since 1949. Waiting eleven years to see a side tour your country heightens anticipation. You don't have that today.

'Also, over the years, South Africa's rugby was pretty similar to ours. Basically they had big men although they were slightly heavier than us and they had some lively backs. For a long time, New Zealand and South Africa were the two dominant teams of world rugby and there wasn't much between us. But the Springboks have fallen off the pace a little in recent times. Yet the quality and depth in South African rugby and knowledge of the game is still very deep there. I have no doubt at all they will re-emerge as one of the top two or three nations in quite a short time. There is such a great appetite for the game when you go there.

'When I look back on my times playing against South Africa, I think the travel is always uppermost in my mind. There were long distances to travel, great sights to see. But it was always a bit wearying, too, because after the long journeys you met another team filled from their endless supply of very tough rugby players. When you are playing thirty-six games you find that difficult and it was very hard to sustain that level over a period of time. Even the midweek games were tough. Of the thirty players we took, usually at least five were injured and that put added pressure on us all.

'But I have wonderful memories of the hospitality we received in South Africa.'

The Southern Hemisphere

Since the first meeting between these two powerful rugby nations of the southern hemisphere in 1921 in Dunedin, South Africa had been superior. But now, in 1956 they had to go to New Zealand, that faraway country known as 'the land of the long white cloud' and the All Blacks were ready for them. They met four times on that tour, in Dunedin, Wellington, Christchurch and Auckland, and there was never more than 7 points between them. New Zealand won the first Test 10-6, South Africa the second, 8-3. The All Blacks took the third, 17-10 and then the fourth, 11-5. It was a contest of seismic proportions in which safety for life and limb rarely entered the equation. This represented the ultimate contest for southern hemisphere

The 1953 New Zealand All Blacks perform the traditional Maori 'Haka' dance.

bragging rights, for Australia was still something of a rugby backwater. At times, it was brutal, a point New Zealand prop Mark Irwin emphasized many years later when the remaining members of that 1956 team came together in Wellington, New Zealand in 2006, to commemorate that historic series.

Irwin condemned those South Africans as 'over physical and guilty of tarnishing their own image'.

He told me: 'They were a physically intimidating, aggressive outfit, there was no doubt about that. To an unacceptable degree at times, I'm afraid. I think they overdid it a bit in that series. I got some thumps in my ribs that were broken in the first Test. What broke them? A tackle, a knee, a punch? I don't know what hit me but it broke some ribs and was very painful.

'They rather spoilt and tarnished their image by being too physical. So it was good to beat them in the series. We felt better about it after that.'

Nevertheless, Irwin still conceded to a grudging admiration for his foes of all those years ago. 'You had to work half as hard again to get equal amounts of possession in the forwards, when you played them. You had to really concentrate on your scrummaging techniques otherwise you would get pushed all over the field.

'I think those were the two things about facing them. Combating their forward strength and power was essential so one could get adequate possession.

'The 1956 Springboks were the best, the strongest I ever played against, better than their 1960 side even though the latter beat us 2-1 in the Test series in South Africa. They had a stronger forward pack in 1956 and their backs were just a shade better, too. They were an excellent side and I thought they didn't need to overdo the physical stuff, which they did. To me, it was needless.'

By 1956, Australia had played South Africa thirteen times since the opening of sporting hostilities between those nations in 1933, and lost ten. The Wallabies' status in the world game was epitomized by the fact that British and Irish touring teams heading to New Zealand traditionally stopped off in Australia for a few warm-up matches. True, the Tests were real contests, the Wallabies winning the occasional one. But no one was in the slightest doubt that the serious stuff really started when they crossed the Tasman Sea.

The official programme for the 1955 England v France game at Twickenham.

The Northern Hemisphere

Undeniably, the rugby of the 1950s was played with a fierce pride and determination. But what hallmarked this glorious, golden era was the sense of fun, the mischievous jokes that accompanied the serious stuff, especially in the northern hemisphere. In Cardiff one year, as Wales and Ireland prepared for a Five Nations Championship match, Irish centre Cecil Pedlow stuck his head out of his jersey in the changing room as they prepared for the match, turned to his old friend Tony O'Reilly and cracked, 'Do you know Reilly, this will be our eighth successive defeat together.'

Then there was the Irish fly-half Mickey English of the Limerick Bohemians club who went to Paris in April 1958 for the final game of that year's Championship. Ireland had already lost to England and Wales, although they did beat the Scots in Dublin.

Ireland's captain that day, Noel Henderson, called his men to order in the dressing room well before the start to make an important announcement. 'Now men' he explained, 'we have a special guest who would like to wish you all the best today.' And into the changing room walked Sir Bernard Law Montgomery, 'Monty' of Second World War fame.

The little man with the smartly clipped moustache went around the room, shaking hands and offering a few words of motivation. When he reached the team's fly-half, he had something of a shock awaiting him.

'Hello, Montgomery of Alamein,' he said to Mickey English to which Ireland's finest shot back, 'English o'Limerick, how's yerself?'

Even the renowned Montgomery was lost for words at that response.

That was a match of famous landmarks. Irish prop Syd Millar from the Ballymena club, made his debut, the prelude to a long and distinguished career not just as a player, but as coach for Ireland and the 1974 British and Irish Lions and then as chairman of the International Rugby Board.

As Millar started, so a great Frenchman Maurice Prat, brother of the immortal Jean, played his twenty-second and final game for France.

The first half of the 1950s had been dominated by Wales. They won the Five Nations Championship five times in seven seasons (1950, 1952, 1954, 1955 and 1956) because they had the tough, tight forwards in men like Rhys Williams, Clem Thomas, Billy Williams and Rhys Stephens. Their renowned front row of W. O. G. Williams, B. V. Meredith and C. C. Meredith, sounded, someone joked, like a firm of solicitors: Williams, Meredith & Meredith.

> 'Do you know Reilly, this will be our eighth successive defeat together.'

In those days, Wales could mine their hard, tough-as-iron forwards from a rich seam at the local colliery and steelworks. All Wales needed then was the backs to complete the job because, for sure, they would get plenty of ball from so strong a pack. In men like Jack Matthews, Bleddyn Williams, Lewis Jones, Cliff Morgan, Ken Jones, Rex Willis, Onllwyn Brace and others they had class oozing from every pore, players of pace and exquisite talent who could cut apart an opposition defence like a child with scissors and paper.

In 1950, Wales's Championship was gilded by a first Grand Slam since 1911. Not until 1957 would Wales' obvious superiority be broken. Surprisingly, it was England who did it, winning the Championship in 1953 but then, much more importantly, landing the Grand Slam in 1957, their first since 1928. For a country with England's playing resources, that was a shocking indictment of its total failure to instil organization, a coherent selection policy and some kind of serious club-playing programme whereby the players could be tested. By contrast, Wales enjoyed a fiercely competitive, vibrant club scene that asked questions of its players whenever they pulled on the jersey of their local team. Anyone from an English club

Following pages: French international Michel Celaya can be seen in the thick of the action in this contest between the French Army and a select South-West France team in April 1955.

crossing the Severn Bridge in a westerly direction and finding themselves at places like Swansea, Cardiff, Newport, Llanelli, Pontypool, Abertillery or Neath knew what to expect. That tough preparation each week readied the top Welsh players for international rugby, whereas England's players might have a couple of relatively competitive games a month interspersed by two absurdly one-sided encounters. Amazingly, this was a problem England would struggle to come to terms with for another thirty years. Indeed, it wasn't really until the late 1980s when leagues were at last introduced into the English club scene, that things began to change.

Then there were the farcical selections and overt favouritism of the England selectors. In 1955, Englishman Dickie Jeeps had been considered good enough to become first choice scrum-half in all four Test matches for the British and Irish Lions. Not only that, he excelled with Cliff Morgan as his half-back partner and impressed everyone with his courage, doughty abilities and service.

Alas, the England selectors knew better. Jeeps, uncapped prior to that tour, played only one Test of the 1956 Five Nations Championship and it wasn't until the following year that he won another cap.

England were Five Nations Champions in 1953, Triple Crown winners (and Championship runners-up) in 1954, runners-up again in 1956, Champions and Grand Slam winners in 1957 and Champions again in 1958. As with Wales, they had built their sustained meritocracy on the backs of some outstandingly talented players, the likes of centres Jeff Butterfield and W. P. C. Davies, wings Peter Jackson and Peter Thompson, scrum-half Jeeps plus forwards like Eric Evans, Ron Jacobs, David Marques and John Currie at lock forward and fine back-row players like Alan Ashcroft, Reg Higgins and 'Tug' Wilson.

> 'For Christ's sake, Pete – I'm on duty and I'm trying to follow someone.'

In 1955 against France at Twickenham, England included Wilson, a London police officer, and Peter Yarranton, the Wasps forward, in their side. The build-up to the game in the early part of the week contained an unusual incident.

Yarranton was strolling down a London street on the Tuesday evening, with some friends, after a few beers in a local hostelry. The boys were in fine fettle: Yarranton was playing against France on Saturday, the beer had been good and all seemed right with the world. Although it was dark, Yarranton cast his gaze across the street and, lo and behold, who was there in the shadows but Tug Wilson, with whom he would play for his country four days later in the international.

'I started waving and shouting across the street to Tug, but found it most odd – he completely ignored me,' Yarranton told me, years later. 'So, like all good Englishmen who cannot make themselves heard, I shouted louder: "Tug, Tug; how are you".' At which point Wilson came scuttling across the street, rushed up to Yarranton and said, 'For Christ's sake, Pete, shut up – I'm on duty and I'm trying to follow someone!'

Someone who was to become rather well known in British political life in later years, Denis Thatcher, husband of Conservative Prime Minister Margaret Thatcher, was one of the touch judges for the 1956 Five Nations Championship match in

Paris between France and England. Thatcher was a keen rugby supporter and official and enjoyed the game throughout his life. By then, rugby matches were being shown live on French television, albeit in a grainy black and white. Camera angles, of course, bore little relation to contemporary times.

By contrast with the achievements of Wales and England, Scotland had a miserable time of it for most of the 1950s. They started, shall we say, inauspiciously, thrashed 44-0 by South Africa at Murrayfield in 1951, a result that stunned the entire rugby-playing world. Incidentally, it was on that tour that the Springbok Basil Kenyon was gouged in an eye during a match in Wales. Sadly, he never played top-class rugby again.

That year, Scotland finished fourth in the Five Nations Championship and then ended up bottom for the next three years running. In 1955, they ended up third, only to fail again in the following years: fourth in 1957 and 1958, bottom in 1956 and 1959.

1958 saw two important events. The law was changed so that a player no longer needed to play the ball with his foot after a tackle. And in June 1958, France went to South Africa and for the first time won a Test series against the mighty Springboks. One South African newspaper had referred to the French disparagingly as men who were 'small and drink two litres of wine a day.' Both may have been true but the South Africans were unwise to write off France that easily. After all, in Paris in 1954, they had beaten New Zealand 3-0, although as one newspaper wrote afterwards 'It was a victory without the ball'.

What the French also had on that tour of South Africa was characters, jokers in their midst. Centre Guy Stener from the Paris University Club (PUC, pronounced 'puke' to generations of schoolboys) played in both Tests against the Springboks and pulled the best con of the whole trip on his pals.

As their aeroplane trundled on somewhere over Africa and most of the players tried to sleep, the wily Stener noted their slumbers and launched into a sudden, noisy shout of excitement. 'Look boys,' he said, 'there's someone selling *L'Equipe* (the famous French daily sports paper) down there'. Stener's pals, thinking they were about to land and almost down, pulled themselves together and rapidly sat bolt upright to be confronted by a sight of desert about 30,000 feet below. A volley of cushions hit Stener amidships.

Thus, no-one took the slightest notice when full-back Pierre Lacaze announced a short time later that an engine had stopped. *Bien sur, bien sur* they smiled, knowingly. Except that, it had. And when a second one failed, the pilot of the jet decided they had to lose height, limp along just above the desert and try to reach Kano, in Nigeria. When they did, the plane came in onto a runway lined by fire engines, always a reassuring sight for those on board. When they finally got off into temperatures of 100 degrees Fahrenheit, they were told they'd be there for two days awaiting another plane. Travel in the 1950s …

France travelled with some heavy emotional baggage to declare: they'd been flogged 25-3 by the Springboks in Paris six years earlier. When they arrived on South African soil, they set their jaws in steely resolve that this time it would be different.

The official programme for the joint teams of England & Wales against Scotland & Ireland in the 1959 Twickenham Jubilee match.

Opposite: France's Pierre Tarricq tackles Ireland scrum-half Andy Mulligan in the 1958 France v Ireland international at Stade Colombes, Paris.

Both Jean and Maurice Prat had gone into retirement but now came Lucien Mias's great moment.

Of course, the tour proceeded with the usual calm to be expected of a French rugby trip. After one match, the Afrikaans newspaper *Die Landstem* reported: 'The whole affair had more right in a boxing ring than on a rugby field. The Frenchmen's dirty play not only lost them the match but resulted in a touring team being booed off the field for the first time in the history of South African rugby.'

But Mias, who was known as 'The Doctor of the Pack', was concerned only with the great scalp of the Springboks. Whatever it would take, he was prepared to do it. Mias was a remarkable character; a strong powerful figure who was the antithesis of authority. It is said the night before the decisive second Test in Johannesburg, he drank half a bottle of rum and was seen wandering drunk around the team's hotel. Some preparation for the Test ... but some result by the end of the next afternoon.

France won, 9-5, to seal their first ever triumph over South Africa. That six-week tour, with all its attendant dramas, boyish japes and exploding human emotions, was immortalized in an outstanding book written by the brilliant French rugby writer Denis Lalanne, entitled *Le Grand Combat au XV de France* (*The Great fight of the French Fifteen*). Lalanne's superb book is a revealing commentary of rugby football in those times.

France had long been almost a law unto themselves. In 1931, they had been banished from the Five Nations Championship due to the whiff of payment to leading players in their country. This hoary old chestnut had appeared with regularity: 'all nonsense, not true Monsieur' in the words of Frenchmen, but 'they've always paid players, those Froggies' in the opinion of the suspicious English and Celts.

Quiet, diplomatic entreaties to the Fédération Française de Rugby to sort out the problem made no discernible difference. So France disappeared from the international picture from 1931 to 1947, a long isolation that bred years of lingering frustration within French rugby circles and was an increasing loss to the Five Nations tournament.

With the ending of the Second World War and the fact that England and France had even been able to come together to fight a war, the rugby authorities clearly felt some sort of fresh start had to be made, post 1945. So France was welcomed back into the fold in 1947. Alas, it didn't take long for the old tales of payment to players to resurface and reach the ears of the IRB members who ran the game with the disdain of Emperors. Accordingly, the French were warned in 1952, warned again twelve months later and warned a final time in 1958. After which, the IRB quietly buried the issue and let Frenchmen do what Frenchmen wanted to do. Anyone who thought that money was not greasing Gallic palms was either a born-again optimist or very wet behind the ears.

But what France also had in the 1950s were some outstandingly talented, distinguished players who lifted the French international game to new levels. In 1952, Guy Basquet, the strong Agen No. 8 who had been a driving force in improving 'Les Tricoleurs' to the point where they were serious challengers for

the Championship, retired after a distinguished career of 33 caps spanning eight seasons. Then came the great Jean Prat who won a remarkable 51 caps from 1945 to 1955, an extraordinary total for those days.

Prat was a legend in his playing days and, in retirement, became revered throughout the land as a colossus of the sport. When he died, in his beloved Lourdes, in 2005, almost the entire town not to mention rugby men from all over France, turned out for his funeral. He had given French rugby great presence.

When he had retired, the role of 'Le Général' passed to the great Lucien Mias and it fell to that fine forward from the Mazamet club to lead France to their first ever Five Nations Championship title in 1959.

They'd been trying, on and off, since 1910 and even though they lost to Ireland and drew with England, victories over Scotland and Wales were enough to give them their triumph.

Nowadays, French club rugby is dominated by a small handful of clubs, most notably Biarritz, Toulouse and Stade Français. On the next level down you find the likes of Perpignan, Agen, Bourgoin and Clermont Auvergne. But take a look at some of the clubs whose players made up France's 1954 winning team against Scotland: FC Lourdes, Racing Club de France, CS Bourg, US Bressane, US Cognac, Aviron Bayonnais, Tarbes and Vienne. Many of them have now virtually disappeared, or are no longer anywhere near the top flight.

Yet Lourdes was once pre-eminent as the most powerful club in France, certainly of the 1950s. They won the coveted French Championship title, the 'Bouclier de Brennu', in 1952, 1953, 1956, 1957, 1958 and 1960, as well as being runners-up in 1955. Lourdes had the great players of the age, like the wonderfully talented Prat brothers, Jean and Maurice, Jean Barthe, Roger Martine, Henri Domec, André Labazuy, Pierre Lacaze and others. These were players of consummate skills and talent, men who had learned the essential basics of the game as youngsters in their local French communities and moved seamlessly into top-class rugby. They brought a great style, a panache to the game in France and indeed, wherever they played.

Whatever their proclivities off the field, the French added immensely to the colour and gaiety of the old Championship. When they were in the mood, they played rugby to make the gods smile, the ball flashing down a three-quarter line where *vitesse, vitesse, plus de vitesse* was the critical factor. None of the French wings had greater gas than Alain Porthault of the suitably named Racing Club de France, who played international rugby for three seasons from 1951 to 1953. Porthault was so fast he was a semi-finalist in the 100m at the Youth Olympics in Helsinki.

Teams visiting Paris generally had the time of their lives on a Saturday evening at the after-match banquet. Indeed, the Irish pair Tony O'Reilly and Andy Mulligan decided after a match there one year that the girls looked so pretty, the spring sunshine was so warm and beguiling and the hospitality so omnipresent that they should stay on for a few days, which they promptly did. These are pleasures denied to the later generations of players.

The official programme for the 1959 match between Blackheath and a star-studded Barbarians team.

Opposite: France captain Jean Prat, nicknamed 'Mr Rugby' by the English press after the first French win at Twickenham in 1951. The flanker, who could kick exceptionally well, won 51 caps, 17 as captain, between 1945 and 1955.

Sir Anthony O'Reilly

Ireland 1955–70

Centre and Wing

Tony O'Reilly won 29 caps for Ireland between 1955 and 1970, mainly as a centre, but it was as a wing for the British & Irish Lions, first in South Africa in 1955 and in New Zealand four years later, that he played his greatest rugby. By a long distance, he remains the Lions' leading try scorer, and scored six in his ten Tests as a Lion.

'In 1959 we could easily have won the Test series 3-1. But in the first Test we had a referee who gave an appalling performance. He was basically incompetent, but we have to remember he was the home referee in that region. So we lost to six penalty goals despite scoring four tries. Yet on modern-day scoring we would have won 25-18, a point of which I always remind Sir Wilson Whineray, one of our opponents that day, when I see him!

Those were times of fun and friendship. But also ferocity, too, occasionally. We had some marvellous players in that era; that was what made it special. On the 1955 tour there was the magic of Cliff Morgan, which can never be forgotten. He was probably the best fly-half ever to leave these shores, with Jack Kyle (who toured New Zealand in 1950) his co-equal. On the hard grounds of Africa, Morgan was fantastic.

We had such fun on that tour and we just ran and ran for five months; that's what I remember. We also used the little kick over the top of the defence or the grubber kick through to make our opponents turn and defend. I wonder why players don't use those tactics far more to defeat the rush defence in the modern-day game for there is much room to be exploited behind that on-rushing defence.

We were the first Lions team to tour there since 1938 and the interest was enormous. But the hard grounds certainly suited our style of play.

New Zealand in 1959 was very different. It was often rainy and the wet and the mud slowed our game down. We were introduced to a style of New Zealand play very much more concentrated on forwards than anything we had seen in South Africa or Australia. Colin Meads typified that.

Opposite: A young Tony O'Reilly lines up before one of his early games for Ireland.

Tony O'REILLY

Tony O'REILLY

I remember the New Zealand Rugby Union President Gordon Brown attempting to defend their win with all those penalties at a tumultuous dinner in Dunedin after the first Test. It was one of the worst nights for New Zealand rugby; we should have won and most New Zealanders were ashamed to see their team win. But Brown said at the dinner they had won "within the framework of the rules" and that became a catchphrase (and excuse) for any sort of jocularity on the remainder of our tour. Even if questioned by our officials for a few incidents, we would repeat the mantra, "But we did it within the framework of the rules". It produced no end of fun.

I would say the most gifted Lions teams I have seen would be our 1955 side in South Africa and the 1971 team in New Zealand. The 1959 Lions would be close to them and, of course, the 1974 Lions were undefeated in South Africa, which was a fine achievement. Perhaps they lacked the skill and verve in the back line. But those sides would have to be the best of that century. In 1971 and 1974 you have to say there was a bit more attrition than in my day, perhaps warfare in 1974 in South Africa.

So although I would doff my hat to certain members of the 1950 Lions such as Jack Kyle, Lewis Jones, Bleddyn Williams and Jack Matthews, I believe the 1955 and 1971 Lions were the best. Barry John and Gareth Edwards were a remarkable pair of half-backs on the 1971 tour but I wouldn't put them ahead of our 1955 halves, Dickie Jeeps and Cliff Morgan.

The great thing about the current Irish squad is that they actually have about twenty players of real international calibre. Strength in depth is crucial, absolutely critical in the modern game, and this Irish squad is terrific in that respect. I am lost in admiration for their overall quality and strength.

Ronan O'Gara's kicking is brilliant, quite exceptional. Then you have the incredible work rate of Brian O'Driscoll. What is so wonderful about him is that his attacking play is so exceptionally good yet even without the ball, O'Driscoll is a heroic defender.

As for the forwards, Ireland has the outstanding Paul O'Connell in the second row. He is, arguably, the finest all-round lock in world rugby. He represents all the virtues of Irish forward play. He is one of the best Irish locks I have ever seen. Robin Thompson, who captained the 1955 Lions, Willie John McBride and Moss Keane were all fine locks, but O'Connell is terrific.

Opposite: Tony O'Reilly on a typically determined run for the British & Irish Lions.

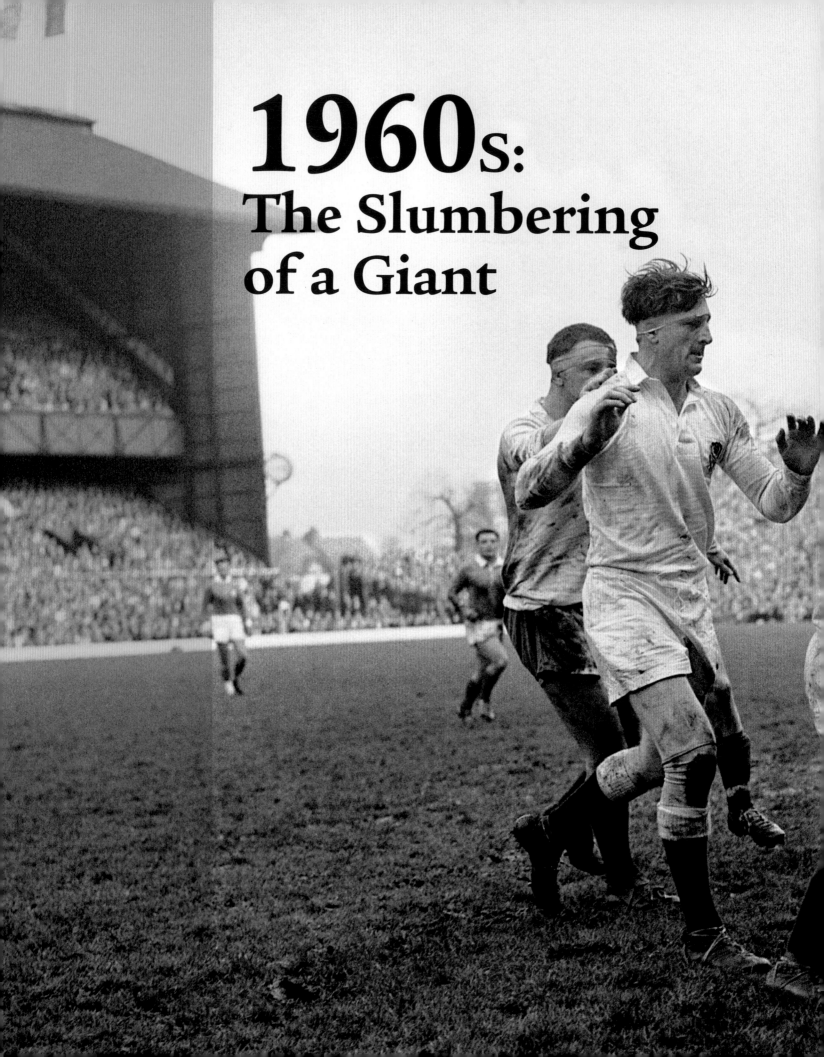

1960s:
The Slumbering of a Giant

1960s: The Slumbering of a Giant

All kinds of weird and wonderful things happened to rugby players of this era.

Take Ireland and Lions lock forward Tom Reid on a Barbarians tour of Canada. On the final evening of the tour, Reid could not be found anywhere. Eventually, early the next morning and only a short while before departure for the airport, Reid's room-mate decided to end a long, wearying night of celebrations and go and pack. Alas, his hotel-room door was barred. From inside. The only response to some loud banging on the door was the creaking of bedsprings. Reid's pal decided help was required.

Thus, a delegation of three of the finest rugby players of that time arrived outside the door: Cliff Morgan of Wales, Tony O'Reilly and Andy Mulligan of Ireland. The trio informed Reid through the closed door that he had to open it and be ready to head for the airport.

Presently, the door was unlocked and opened as far as the night security chain would permit. O'Reilly takes up the tale. 'There stood Reid clad only in his parish priest socks and, as Mulligan memorably remarked, "with obvious signs of human passion about his person".'

The door was forced open, upon which act Reid hopped back into bed alongside a blond girl.

'Come on you silly bugger, we've got a plane to catch', he was told.

'I'm not coming home, I'm staying. I'm in love and getting married, that's it,' he told his bemused pals. And he did. Three times, actually. And so ended, prematurely, one of the great international careers of the time.

The Lions Lose their Roar

In the northern hemisphere, the 1960s continued in a similar vein. Players still had fun and still spent eighty minutes playing a club match as an excuse for standing in the bar afterwards drinking for six or seven hours.

The returning Lions of 1955 and 1959 had revealed to the countries of Britain and Ireland the standards operating in the southern hemisphere. The seriousness with which rugby was approached in those countries was the complete opposite to the laissez-faire approach on the other side of the world.

The variance in the two attitudes meant that in the 1960s the Lions did not win a single Test match of the twelve they played against South Africa and New Zealand. It was a catastrophic run.

In 1962, the Lions, led by the brilliant, highly intelligent Scottish wing Arthur Smith, went to South Africa and in truth, came within a whisker of success. They drew the first Test in Johannesburg 3-3, but then narrowly lost the next two, 3-0 in

Previous pages: France's Michel Crauste grapples for the ball with England's Ron Jacobs.

Durban and 8-3 in Cape Town. Only in the fourth Test was there a hammering, 34-14, on Bloemfontein's hard, unrelenting concrete-like ground.

The problem of local refereeing again reared its contentious head in Durban. The Lions appeared to score a perfectly good try in the last minute of the game through their lock forward Keith Rowlands. That would have tied the scores at 3-3 with the conversion to come, and a chance for the Lions to win the game. Rowlands got up in some glee until he saw the referee Ken Carlson refuse to award the score, claiming he was 'unsighted'. This was not the first time that a southern hemisphere referee had disallowed an apparently valid, match-winning try when the Lions looked like they might beat the locals. It became a sad and sick joke and ultimately forced the International Rugby Board to introduce neutral referees, a move resisted for years by countries like South Africa and New Zealand. There were plenty of examples to understand why.

The 1962 Lions did not lack talent. In players like Smith, David Hewitt, Ken Jones, Dewi Bebb, Dickie Jeeps, Gordon Waddell, Bryn Meredith, Syd Millar, Alan Pask and Budge Rogers, they had plenty of ability. But more of those by now familiar selectorial

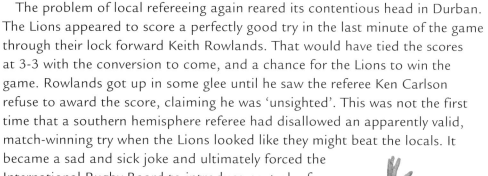

The Lions and South Africa contest a line-out ball on their tour of South Africa in 1962.

aberrations undermined their ambitions and the tour, in terms of results, failed.

Four years later, it was said that the painful lessons learned from previous Lions failures had been heeded. Thus, the 1966 tour to New Zealand would be different, but anyone who believed the 1966 Lions rugby men would match the achievement of the England football team in winning the soccer World Cup that summer were to be disappointed

In fact, the Lions were so outclassed that that they were whitewashed 4-0 in the Test series, lost four provincial games and could only draw two others. All this despite the encouragement of a stop-over in Australia where they won seven of their eight matches including both Tests against the Wallabies. The other was drawn.

It seemed to augur well for the New Zealand tour that followed but as before, the chasm in standards between the two hemispheres was to be cruelly emphasized. Once again, it wasn't as though the Lions didn't have any players. In men like Ray McLoughlin, Keith Rowlands, David Nash, Bill Mulcahy, Bryn Meredith, Mike Gibson, David Watkins, Willie John McBride, Dewi Bebb, Stewart Wilson, Alan Pask and Stuart Watkins, there was considerable talent. Indeed, some thought this was the young Gibson's greatest Lions tour and McLoughlin was one of the best scrummagers of any era. The trouble was, there weren't enough class operators or men of sufficiently deep determination to take the fight to the All Blacks in their country. As Willie John McBride said, 'The tour was undermined even before the squad met up because plainly, there were players included who simply were not up to the task of taking on the All Blacks in their own backyard. The whole composition of the touring party and also the attitude was wrong.'

'Kicks on the head ... or broken noses ... do not come under the heading of hard play, to which no rugby man objects. Instead, they are just plain dirty.'

What the Lions couldn't handle was the mental intensity of the gruelling thirty-five-matches of the tour or the physical excesses of the New Zealand rugby men. It had been the same in South Africa four years earlier when the Springbok flanker Mannetjies Roux had smashed the cheekbone of the Lions fly-half Richard Sharp in the provincial match against Northern Transvaal, forcing Sharp out of the first two Tests.

In New Zealand four years later, the Lions found similarly distasteful acts for which they were unprepared. Vivien Jenkins, the *Sunday Times* rugby writer of the era, complained: 'Competition taken to the extreme, as it is in New Zealand, produces things that, to our own players, are not worth the ends involved. Dirty play is one of them and there was more than enough of this on tour. Kicks on the head which necessitate stitches or broken noses from stiff arm tackles do not come under the heading of hard play, to which no rugby man objects. Instead, they are just plain dirty. No doubt we will be accused of squealing, the usual New Zealand comeback, but the only alternative is to stay silent and respond in kind, and what kind of a game does that make rugby?'

What Jenkins did not know was that some members of the Lions touring party

Opposite: A Lion and Springbok wrestle to the delight and shock of the Durban crowd. The touring Lions lost to the South African side by one penalty after having a match-winning try controversially disallowed.

were making a mental note that the only way to survive this roughhouse approach was to adopt similar tactics. This would become clear in time.

As McBride added: 'They [New Zealand] played the game hard and with a single ambition, to win. Nothing else mattered. Hands were stood on, limbs broken, fists smashed into Lions faces; it was all seen as part of the game. I knew from my own experiences in facing the All Blacks in 1963 [in Dublin] what to expect, but some of my Lions colleagues seemed surprised and dismayed. Worse still, they began to disappear when the rough stuff started and the punishment was being dished out.'

McBride copped some of the treatment straight from the kick-off in one provincial match. He caught the ball and was immediately engulfed by four or five members of the opposing pack who drove him 30 yards downfield, kicking, punching and giving him a fearful physical hammering. When the whistle eventually went to end his torment, McBride was still holding onto the ball – 'I wasn't going to let those bastards have it' – but his Lions colleagues were 20 yards away, laughing to themselves.

'Why didn't you let the bastards have it?' said one.

Colin Meads, a man not renowned for holding back in the tackle, displays the All Blacks determination. Lions full-back Stewart Wilson is his victim.

'I knew in that moment from that single remark, we had no chance in the Test series,' said the great Irishman. 'It was obvious our players weren't prepared to take the pain. Only a few of our players felt like I did. I got bloody annoyed at the lack of desire and determination to stand up to the All Blacks on the field.'

One of the forwards on that tour was Wales second row Brian Price, a man regarded as one of the toughest in the old Five Nations Championship. Price had been playing international rugby since 1961 and should have been a key man on that 1966 Lions trip. After all, he'd been a member of the Newport team that had upset the 1963 New Zealand touring team with a 3-0 victory at Rodney Parade, their only defeat of that momentous 1963/4 tour.

But when Price got to New Zealand with the Lions, he found Colin Meads targeting him. The response from the Welshman was limp – 'he seemed content to melt into the background and lose his Test place,' McBride claimed. The Irishman further alleged: 'Price didn't play for some time and I suspect much of it was because Meads had got to him.'

Prior to 1966, the touring Lions party had never had a formal coach. But this time they appointed a Welshman John Robins to fill the role alongside an Irish manager, Des O'Brien. Alas, neither man really covered himself in glory. Robins injured an Achilles and couldn't do much; O'Brien's decision to fly off to Fiji for a holiday during the tour to alleviate some of the stress under which he laboured, was greeted with astonishment by the hard-nosed New Zealanders.

'It was obvious our players weren't prepared to take the pain. Only a few players felt like I did.'

As ever, preparations were at best haphazard. Before the first Test in Dunedin, the touring party was split into two, the Test team heading for Queenstown, the famous ski resort in New Zealand's south island, and the rest further down the coast to Dunedin. Willie John McBride remembers receiving a light-hearted call from his (injured) fellow Irishman Ray McLoughlin, enquiring, 'How's your tour going up there in the mountains?'

Not well, was the answer. For winter snow in the resort, not exactly an unknown occurrence, had prevented the Test team from doing any serious practice. But wonder of wonders, after some days of frustration and players gingerly walking around on the ice-and snow-covered streets, news came that a green swathe of land had been discovered where the tourists could hone their skills in readiness for the Saturday Test match.

Alas, as with most things attached to Lions tours in those days, it proved a false dawn of hope. No sooner had the tourists started work on the lush grass than a cry went up, 'Incoming flight'. At which point, they had to grab the loose rugby balls lying around and rush into a nearby hangar for shelter. Air New Zealand flight 51 from Christchurch was about to land at Queenstown airport, where the Lions were trying to train.

The Dunedin Test was lost, conclusively, 20-3. Another defeat followed, 16-12, in Wellington, a match for which the Lions captain Mike Campbell-Lamerton was dropped, an almost unknown humiliation for a Lions skipper. Lancaster Park, Christchurch, brought no change in the third Test, the All Blacks winning 19-6, and they completed the clean sweep with a 24-11 victory in the fourth and final Test in Auckland.

The final Lions series of the 1960s was back in South Africa in 1968. This tour was to become arguably the most hilarious, the most convivial and the most outrageous of all Lions tours in history. At one point, en route by train from Johannesburg to Nelspruit, jumping off point for the Kruger National Park where the Lions were to spend a few days relaxing and viewing the animals, a riotous party ensued. Players were turned out of their beds in the dead of night as whooping, hollering young rugby men went storming down the train corridors shouting and screaming.

Unfortunately, innocent passengers became caught up in the mêlée, to which some, not surprisingly, objected. The consequence was that at some point in the night, in a country station, the Lions' carriage was disconnected from the train and left in the sidings. There, the rabble was left to sleep off their excesses.

Whilst all this was going on under the management of the Harlequins official

Members of the 1968 Lions touring team practise their scrum-half passing during a training session at Eastbourne. Roger Young, Gareth Edwards and Billy Raybould are the men hurling the balls.

David Brooks, a man to whom partying was as endemic a part of life as eating, the Lions were doing what their forebears had done earlier in the decade: lose the Test series. They went down 25-20 in Pretoria, but managed a 6-6 draw at Port Elizabeth in the second Test to keep the series alive. Alas, they were defeated 11-6 in Cape Town in the third Test, which meant the series was lost, and then 19-6 in Johannesburg in the fourth Test.

It completed a grim era for the Lions. Of twelve Test matches contested in the 1960s in South Africa and New Zealand, the two countries where the world's real power resided, they lost ten and drew two. It was an appalling indictment of muddled planning, absurd tolerance of the principle of fun over anything else and a revealing comment on the priorities that still prevailed at that time in northern hemisphere rugby.

Men like Willie John McBride confessed: 'After making those three Lions tours, I returned home wondering whether I could face any more. The thought of any more such experiences in South Africa and New Zealand was too much to stomach. Mentally, I made a private decision never to go back.'

Nor were things very different for the individual countries of the northern hemisphere when they ventured south of the Equator. England played the All Blacks four times in the 1960s and lost the lot: 21-11 and then 9-6 on their 1963 tour, 14-0 and 23-11 when the New Zealanders came to Twickenham in 1964 and 1967.

A cartoon in the New Zealand *Evening Post* in June 1963 after England had lost both Test matches on their short tour to the country, showed an England player, suitcase in hand, walking away with torn clothing and bruises all over his body. A New Zealand forward is saying to him, 'And don't forget to tell 'em over there what they have got coming to 'em.'

After the All Blacks had demolished England 14-0 at Twickenham on that 1963/4 tour, a headline in a London newspaper said: 'All Blacks a team of men among boys' and 'Too fit, too fast, too fiery for England XV'. Truth was, New Zealand's players had a greater physicality, were faster, fitter and much better prepared.

Programme for the final England trial match at Twickenham, December 1966.

'After making those three Lions tours, I returned home wondering whether I could face any more.'

Poles Apart

The trend of the all-conquering southern hempisphere teams continued. Against South Africa, England fared slightly better, losing 5-0 in 1961 but managing an 11-8 win in 1969, both at Twickenham. Against the so-called 'weaker' Australians, England went down 18-9 at Sydney in 1963 and 23-11 at Twickenham in 1967.

Wales weren't much better. They lost four times to New Zealand in the 1960s, 6-0 in 1963, 13-6 in 1967 and 19-0 and 33-12 on their 1969 tour. South Africa beat them 3-0 in 1960 and 24-3 in 1964, while they also lost, 14-11, to Australia in 1966 before narrowly beating the Wallabies 19-16 in Sydney in 1969.

By contrast, Scotland and Ireland did a little better. The Scots began the decade by losing twice to South Africa, 18-10 in Port Elizabeth in 1960 and 12-5 in Edinburgh the following year. But in 1964, they achieved what no other side managed: they held the touring All Blacks to a 0-0 draw at Murrayfield. The next year they beat South Africa at Murrayfield 8-5 and followed that with a 1966 win over Australia at Murrayfield by 11 points to 5, a distinguished trinity of triumphs. True, New Zealand beat them in Edinburgh on their next tour, 1967, by 14 points to 3, but in 1968 Scotland again toppled the Wallabies, 9-3 in Edinburgh. Finally, in 1969, they again beat the Springboks at Murrayfield, 6-3.

These were encouraging results in the context of the virtual wasteland that was being experienced by the players of England and Wales against southern hemisphere opponents. What is more, Ireland also had some good results.

They had beaten a southern hemisphere nation for the first time in 1958, Australia in Dublin, and although they lost to South Africa in 1960 in Dublin (3-8) and in 1961 in Cape Town (24-8), as well as being narrowly defeated 6-5 by the All Blacks in Dublin in 1963, better things were around the corner.

They beat South Africa 9-6 in Dublin in 1965, then had a hat-trick of wins against the Australians. They won 15-8 in Dublin in 1967, 11-5 in Sydney a few months later and then 10-3 at Lansdowne Road the following year.

What most of these results underlined was the gap that continued to exist between the southern hemisphere major rugby-playing nations and the countries of the northern hemisphere. True, the playing field was slightly evened up when the southern hemisphere countries embarked on their (then) long tours of the UK, Ireland and France. But there was an intensity, a dedication and an importance known to all rugby men in countries like New Zealand and South Africa that simply wasn't the same elsewhere.

The Australians were battling hard to exist so close to the powerful Kiwis, and they unearthed some players of supreme skills in that era, such as half-backs Ken Catchpole and Phil Hawthorne plus Tony Miller, in the pack.

What Vivien Jenkins described as 'competition taken to the extreme' was typified by a trio of incidents involving the legendary New Zealand lock forward Colin Meads in the later years of the 1960s.

In December 1967, playing for New Zealand against Scotland at Murrayfield, Meads was warned in the first half by the Irish referee Kevin Kelleher for dangerous play. But later in the game the All Black appeared to launch a kick that caught Scottish fly-half David Chisholm and was sent off. It was the first dismissal of an All Black since Cyril Brownlee in 1924. Meads was suspended for two tour games but the ignominy was far greater than the short period of absence from the game.

Some New Zealand commentators called it an injustice yet just six months later, in June 1968 whilst playing for the All Blacks against Australia in the first Test at the Sydney Cricket Ground, the brilliant Wallaby scrum-half Ken Catchpole found himself trapped awkwardly in a ruck. Meads unaware of Catchpole's inability to move, grabbed his leg and wrenched it in an effort to

Opposite: 'Mine!' Powerful New Zealand lock Colin Meads grabs the ball, a familiar sight in the 1960s.

The official programme for Gareth Edwards' debut match for Wales against the French in Paris. France won 20-14.

move him off the ball. He literally tore almost all the player's groin muscles to shreds. The screams of agony could be heard in several parts of the ground.

Catchpole had made his international debut in 1961 and by this time was regarded as one of the greatest scrum-halves in the world. He had won 27 caps. Alas, the damage inflicted by Meads's action meant that he never played again. It was a sad, brutal end to a fine international career.

The following year, in May 1969, in the Christchurch Test match between New Zealand and Wales, Meads punched the Welsh hooker Jeff Young so hard that the player's jaw was fractured and he took no further part in the tour.

But Meads knew how to take blows and suffer pain himself. In August 1970, he played a Test match against South Africa in Port Elizabeth with only a protective cast covering his broken arm.

Colin Meads played fifty-five Tests for New Zealand in a career of great longevity spanning the years 1957–71. Today, he is, perhaps only after Sir Wilson Whineray, regarded as the greatest living All Black. But the excesses by which he risked staining his reputation were regarded as justifiable by most New Zealanders. South Africans of that era would also have subscribed to such a viewpoint.

But it was in stark contrast to the opinions existing at the time in the countries of the British Isles and Ireland. Of course, the French could mix it, and often did. Violence frequently marred their matches, with fistfights a feature of games, especially at club level. When local pride was at stake no Frenchman worthy of the name would take a step back. As someone once wrote 'If you want to interest a Frenchman in a game, you tell him it's a war. But if you want to interest an Englishman in a war you tell him it's a game.'

At international level, the French did what they do best: unpredictability. In 1961, on their New Zealand tour, they lost all three Tests, 13-6, 5-3 and a thumping 32-3. Three years later when the countries met again, they lost 12-3 in Paris, and in 1967 on the same Stade Colombes ground, once more went down, 21-15.

Things were more encouraging against the Springboks. The two countries drew 0-0 in Paris in 1961 before France won 8-6 at Springs, on the Eastern Transvaal, in 1964. In 1967, France undertook a four-Test-match tour of South Africa. They lost the first two games, 26-3 in Durban and 16-3 in Bloemfontein. Yet from the ashes of such defeats the French put together a performance good enough to snatch a 19-14 Test win in Johannesburg. The series was still alive as they went to Cape Town for the decider.

Both sides could have won it, but a 6-6 draw meant the Springboks just edged the series. A year later, there was more South African success with Test wins in Bordeaux (12-9) and in Paris, by 16 points to 11.

Matches with Australia provided some solace for France, with Test match victories in 1961 in Sydney, 15–8 points and in Paris in 1967 by 20 points to 14. Australia won 11-10 when the two sides met again in Sydney in 1968.

Interestingly, the emerging Romanians gave France more trouble than Australia in the 1960s, beating them in 1960, 1962 and 1968 and drawing in 1961 and 1963.

Opposite: The colossal French captain Walter Spanghero leading his team out.

The Five Nations Championship

If the 1950s had been Wales's era in the old Five Nations Championship, then it would have been the same in the 1960s, but for one country: France. Between them, the two nations dominated the Championship throughout this decade, winning the title in nine of the ten years. Only England, in 1963, briefly managed to break the monopoly.

As before, substitutions remained a far-off dream. At Murrayfield in January 1960, French wing Lucien Roge broke his hand but had to play on, because no replacements were allowed under the law. France just edged home despite the handicap, 13-11, and in winning three of their four games with the other drawn, took the title.

They retained it the following year, 1961, for the third season in succession, building their success once more around the quality and experience of players like Michel Celaya, François Moncla and Michel Vannier, all of whom featured in

France's Guy Camberabero converts the first French try in a match against England at Twickenham in 1967. France won 16-12 and Camberabero finished the championship with a then record points total of 32.

France's three successive Championship titles. At the end of this season, all three would end their international careers, but France had new men of class and talent waiting to step into their shoes.

For all of the Five Nations competitors it was a time for introducing new caps. In 1960 at Twickenham, England beat Wales 14-6 with a side that contained six backs holding just 14 caps between them. Two years later, Ireland went to Twickenham with an astonishing 9 new caps. They'd been pulling them onto the bus as they drove along the motorway the Irish were building to Twickenham, someone joked. Predictably, Ireland lost 16-0 that day, yet two of the new men, Ray McLoughlin and Willie John McBride, were to become among Ireland's greatest ever forwards. Then, in 1965, the entire cap total for the England side that lost to Ireland in Dublin was just 69 and two years later, England took 8 new caps to Ireland and won, 8-3.

'Out with the old, in with the new,' seemed to be a catchphrase that epitomized the selectors' views at this time.

And Five Nations seasons in those days, in an era of fixture lists uncluttered by too many competitions, just went on and on. The 1960 Championship began on 9 January and did not finish until 9 April, an extraordinary span of over twelve weeks.

1962 saw France retain their title and dominance, a consistency matched only by Ireland's completely contrasting fortunes. Bottom in 1960, 1961 and 1962, they finished second from bottom in 1963 and then bottom again in 1964. It was as well that the Irish retained their sense of humour, on and off the field. Like the front-row forward who went up to his captain during a break in play and angrily thrust his forearm in front of the leader's gaze.

'Look at my arm' he exclaimed, mumbling and spluttering with fury. 'That bastard over there's bitten me.' And sure enough, there were the teeth marks.

His captain looked puzzled.

'Why are you mumbling? And why don't you go and bite him back?', asked the skipper.

'I'd like to,' he replied, 'only, I can't. I've left my false teeth in the changing room.'

And then there was the wizard jape pulled by one London Irish player, Kevin Lavelle, a Royal Navy sailor who found himself marooned one day on the *Ark Royal* in the Bay of Naples. Lavelle was summoned to his captain's cabin and addressed as follows: 'Well now, Lavelle, we have had a request to release you to play rugby for Ireland. Now normally we don't allow this sort of thing, but in the circumstances, we are prepared to do so. Have your bags ready at 0900.'

> 'Why are you mumbling?
> And why don't you go and
> bite him back?'

Lavelle did as he was told. With a smirk on his face.

At 0900, a helicopter landed on deck and whisked him to the nearest air base from where he was flown to London. He went straight to Sunbury-on-Thames, home of London Irish, was royally received and played the club match the following afternoon. A long evening of riotous celebration followed.

Alas, as with all such escapades, there was a price to pay. When the Navy heard the truth, Lavelle was for the high jump. 'I was in irons for a month after they found out,' he told a pal.

'But,' he added, in the spirit of those times, 'it was worth it.'

Watching the French at that time was invariably worth it. If something dazzling and spectacular wasn't happening on the field, it was off it, in the selectors' room. A defeat would bring forth the guillotine and a new bunch thrust into the fray. French selectors played fast and loose with players' careers throughout that era. Yet increasingly, they had the players to try, and a new batch always seemed ready to step up.

As a year, 1963 was an aberration in terms of the total dominance of France and Wales in that decade. It was a suitably bizarre, topsy-turvy Championship. Scotland won in Paris, England in Cardiff, France in Dublin, Wales in Edinburgh and Ireland in Cardiff. At Twickenham in the second half of March, England's attacking fly half

Richard Sharp scored an individual try with a brilliant dummy and scything run that brought the house down, in their 10-8 win. By complete contrast, Wales, who had chosen the Pontypool scrum half Clive Rowlands as captain in his first international against England, went to Murrayfield to play Scotland in February. The diminutive half-back proceeded to kick the life out of the game, playing as though Wales had only a nine-man team with their pack and scrum-half.

It was said afterwards that 105 line-outs were formed, as Rowlands belted the ball into touch whenever he had it. Ultimately, this tour de force, which interested only the statistically minded or the sadists, led to a law change in which no player could kick the ball into touch on the full, if he was outside his own 25-yard line. It was a law of wisdom that freed up the game from the kind of Clive Rowlands-inspired nightmare.

Typically for that time, England won the 1963 Championship on the back of three wins and a draw and then promptly collapsed as a serious rugby power on the international stage. From that high point, they declined so much that they were to win just two of their next seventeen Championship games.

These alarming fluctuations in form by England typified their approach. When they managed, from all their playing resources, to put together a successful team,

England's Richard Sharp kicks downfield after beating a tackle by France's Pierre Lacroix at Twickenham. Michel Crauste (*left*) is too late to reach him.

no one ever thought of building on it so that the success could be sustained. Every season they started afresh, with concomitant chaos and unpredictability in team selection and results.

Wales won the Championship in 1964, on points from a resurgent Scottish side that actually won more matches (three) compared to Wales's two, but suffered a defeat in Cardiff compared to two draws by the Welsh.

But Scotland's bubble, like England's, was to burst all too prematurely. The following year, 1965, they ended up bottom of the Championship as Wales retained their title. As in 1963 when Richard Sharp scored that memorable try at Twickenham against them, another Englishman did even better when the Scots returned to London.

Scotland were leading 3-0 with barely two minutes remaining, with England defending deep in their own 25. England fly-half Mike Weston flung out a hopeful pass to left wing Andy Hancock and the Northampton player set off for the distant Scottish line. He seemed within reach of a couple of Scottish defenders but managed to elude them and as he set sail for glory, a nation's hopes went with him.

France's Christian Carrere prepares to pass in a Five Nations match against Wales, played in difficult conditions in March 1968.

Hancock was no speedster but he set up a steady pace and added a weaving, intricate route to his path. It completely bamboozled the Scottish defence and he eventually collapsed, heaving and huffing from the 75-yard run, over the line. The conversion was missed but the Scots had been denied.

Thoughts that such an inspirational moment might regenerate English rugby proved wildly optimistic. England finished bottom of the pile the next year, 1966, as Wales took the title for the third year in succession. They did it by winning a pulsating match in Cardiff on the last day of the season, defeating France 9-8 after they had trailed 8-0 at one point.

Stuart Watkins's dramatic interception and 65-yard run to the French line turned the game, although there was drama to the last kick when French full-back Claude Lacaze lined up a penalty goal from 48 yards that would have won the match and snatched the Championship title. It was sweetly struck and on target for most of its flight, only to be blown just outside the left-hand post at the last by the strong wind. Wales were Champions.

In 1967, Ireland was captained for the first time in the Championship by flanker Noel Murphy, a (by then) experienced back-row forward who had a wonderful way with words in his team talks. As he prepared to lead his team out of the home dressing room at Lansdowne Road for the game with England in February, Murphy, his face set with determination and seriousness, advised his men, 'Now spread out lads and stick together.' Perhaps it was no wonder England won 8-3.

'Now spread out lads and stick together!'

Injuries continued to cause ridiculous disruption to teams with no replacements allowed. Scotland won 9-8 in Paris, but only after French centre Jo Maso, on his debut, had suffered a bad leg injury and been forced to retire. Nevertheless, from that poor start, France beat England, Wales and Ireland to take the Championship. But 1967 was famous for another moment. Wales went to Paris on 1 April with a team that included a new young scrum-half from the Cardiff Training College. He was still a teenager but his name was destined to go down in the annals of the game as one of the greatest the sport would ever know. Gareth Edwards had arrived and although he couldn't prevent France winning 20-14 at Colombes, the seeds were being sown in the Welsh national team for a glorious new dawn in the 1970s.

Yet it was France who supped the champagne twelve months later by winning the coveted Grand Slam for the first time in their history. But, truth to tell, they stumbled over the finishing line to glory only after the most extraordinary series of selection changes any team can ever have experienced in a single season. The notion that a consistent, settled side is the best bet for success had plainly never entered the heads of the French selectors. Indeed, their taste for blood meant that a remarkable seventeen changes were made in the French team that season alone.

France began by beating Scotland 8-6 at Murrayfield, but the selectors were not impressed. For the next match against Ireland in Paris, out went full-back Claude Lacaze, centre Jo Maso and the little half-back brothers Guy and Lilian

Camberabero, of the La Voulte Sportif club. For the game against Ireland in Paris, Jean-Pierre Lux returned at centre, Jean Gachassin (known as the Peter Pan of French rugby) came in at fly-half, with a new cap at scrum half, J-H. Mir, of Lourdes. Finally, the TOEC back-row player Jean Salut replaced J-J. Rupert.

Alas, France's comfortable 16-6 win was again insufficient for the selectors. This time, they really wielded the axe. Nine changes were made for the game against England in Paris, with Lacaze recalled, Bonal brought in on the wing and Gachassin moved from fly-half to centre. The Camberabero brothers were restored at half-back, a new front row of Lasserre, Yachvili and Noble appeared and Plantefol replaced Dauga at lock. Musical chairs as a party game never knew such unpredictabilties.

France won, 14-9, to keep the Grand Slam in sight, but the familiar guillotine again appeared. Out went Gachassin and Lux with a new centre pair of Maso and

A balletic experience on liquid mud. Christian Carrere and Walter Spanghero look on as France gather the ball against Wales in March 1968.

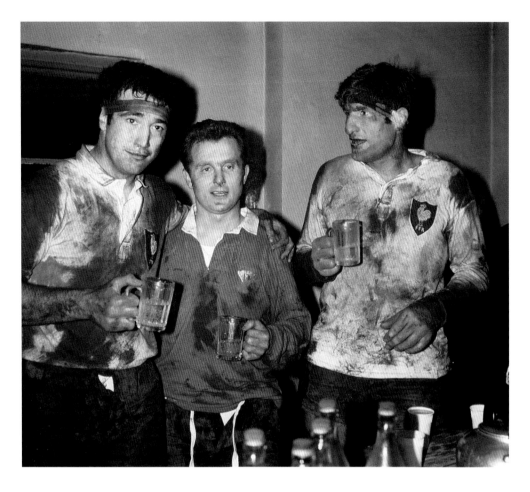

Frenchmen Christian Carrère (left), Guy Camberabero (centre) and Walter Spanghero (right) celebrate the victory over Wales in Cardiff, that set up France's first ever Grand Slam.

Claude Dourthe tried. And the Grenoble back row man Greffe replaced Salut.

In probably any other country such turmoil in selection would almost inevitably have led to chaos and defeat. Not so in France. They promptly beat Wales in Cardiff 14-9, Guy Camberabero (at 5 ft 4 in) and Lilian, his brother (at 5 ft 2in) scoring 11 of their 14 points. It was an astonishing climax to an incredible season for France and the ultimate outcome was that the match winning Camberabero brothers, having masterminded the Grand Slam season, never played for France again! But triumph was tinged with tragedy. Just three months before France's historic first Grand Slam, two of their internationals had been killed in car accidents. The brilliant Guy Boniface, brother of André, died on New Year's Eve 1967 whilst driving home after a club match with Mont-de-Marsan and just three days later, French wing Jean Michel Capendeguy also died in a road accident ten days before he was due to win his second cap for France.

The wonder turned into a wake for France: they finished bottom of the Championship the following season, 1969, as Wales regained top spot. But perhaps most importantly that year, a law change was at last invoked, allowing teams to replace injured players. And the law forbidding players to kick directly into touch apart from in their own 25, resulted in more tries being scored in that year's Championship (32), and more points (234), than at any time in the previous

fifty-eight years. At last, sense had prevailed among the game's lawmakers.

So rugby in the northern hemisphere was keenly contested and often aesthetically exciting. But in that era it was never, ever played with the intensity of Test series between New Zealand and South Africa. These were truly *the* clashes of world rugby.

The Clash of the Titans

In 1960, New Zealand went to South Africa for the return Test series after they had beaten the Springboks for the first time in a series four years earlier. To say that South Africa in 1960 was ready and waiting would be totally wrong: they'd been ready and waiting for four long years. This was a dish of revenge that had been simmering in the pot for one hell of a long time.

The stories that had been told of how New Zealand had brought down the mighty Springboks in 1956, stunning an entire, expectant nation on the southern tip of Africa, had been told over and over. Now came the Springboks' chance to turn the tables, to regain their glory and restore reputations.

So the New Zealanders arrived, all surly expressions and faces set in grim determination. For they, too, had few misapprehensions – their whole country was holding its collective breath, awaiting the outcome. This was more than a series of simple rugby matches; national pride and honour were at stake. No quarter would be asked, nor given.

A young South African back named John Gainsford from Western Province had been chosen for his first international against the touring Scotland team in Port Elizabeth early that season. But nothing, not even the nerves associated with making your Test debut, could have prepared Gainsford for what came next. For only his second cap he was plunged into the cauldron of the first Test of the 1960 series against New Zealand, at Ellis Park, Johannesburg.

John Gainsford was destined to become one of the greatest backs South Africa has ever known. He was strong, quick, clever and creative, a genius of a player who would play for the Springboks from 1960 to 1967 and compile 33 caps, a handsome return for those times that bore testimony to his great class and talent.

But listen to Gainsford's thoughts on that immense contest, between the two most powerful rugby-playing nations in the world. 'You've got to remember that my first thought about international rugby had been in 1949 when Fred Allen's All Blacks had toured our country. The Springboks won that series 4-0 but that statistic didn't tell the true story – in the four Test matches, there was not a single game where the margin between the sides was any more than six points. South Africa won 15-11, 12-6, 9-3 and 11-8. So although South Africa won, we youngsters were in awe of the All Blacks. All we'd had before were pictures of these tremendous men with great power.

'We youngsters were in awe of the All Blacks ... Imagine then my thoughts when I was chosen for only my second cap to play against them.'

Opposite: The mighty South African Springbok John Gainsford.

'Imagine then my thoughts when I was chosen for only my second cap to play against them at the start of that 1960 series. To go on the field against them was awesome. For at least six months before they arrived, the build-up, expectation and excitement was immense. You just wanted to play at that high level.

'The scores give an indication of how close the series was and it was the first time that I understood what international rugby meant. We won the first Test 13-0 but lost the second, 11-3. The third Test at Bloemfontein was drawn 11-all after the All Blacks scored 8 points in the last five minutes. So the series was decided in the last Test, at Port Elizabeth, and it was a hard battle which we just edged 8-3.

'I remember walking with the team to the cinema one evening before one of those Test matches. As we were leaving the hotel, we walked past the New Zealanders who were going somewhere else. Things were so tense, we didn't even greet one another. Not a man on either side raised a 'Hello, how is it going?' or anything like that. You kept your head down and kept walking until you were past them.

'In fact, in 1964 for the South African jubilee when several overseas players were invited to attend, we got to know some of the New Zealanders quite well. So we knew them better when we went to New Zealand for the 1965 series, under the captaincy of Dawie de Villiers. Unfortunately, we lost that series 3-1 and New Zealand's 20-3 win in the final Test at Auckland was their biggest ever over us at that time. They scored five tries to none that day.

'Playing New Zealand was something else, it was so physically hard. You knew you'd had a game of rugby, all right.'

'I would say those four Tests in 1960 were the hardest, the toughest, the most pressurized Test matches I ever played in. It was the most intense rugby you could imagine. When we went to the UK and played all the international teams over there later that year, it was nowhere near as intense. The northern hemisphere teams weren't at the same level; playing New Zealand was something else, it was so physically hard. You knew you'd had a game of rugby, all right. You needed two to three days to get your body together after one of those Tests. It was that hard and tough.

'One match we played on our 1960/61 tour to Britain and Ireland, on the English south coast, left me with an extraordinary memory of rugby in the Britain at that time. We'd been staying at Eastbourne and when we got to the ground, we saw our opponents' coach pull up and they were singing. We were ready to chew leather, bite stones as we'd been used to in the highly physical contests against the All Blacks. But here were our English opponents singing songs in the build-up to a game. We couldn't believe that.

'But the British and Irish sides only used to get together on a Friday and toss the ball around among themselves. Yet they had some great players who could play, as was proven by the fact that we only beat England 5-0, Scotland 12-5, Ireland 8-3 and Wales 3-0, whilst we drew 0-0 with France in Paris. It rather proved that the UK, Irish and French teams did have good players.'

Previous pages: New Zealand scrum-half Kevin Bricoe prepares to off-load possession against the Springboks in 1960.

Opposite: One of the best. New Zealand's Kel Tremain a superb player, kicks as Welsh wing Dewi Bebb tackles.

Jean-Pierre Lux

France 1967–75

Wing and Centre

Jean-Pierre Lux made his international rugby debut for France in 1967 and won 47 caps before his retirement in 1975. He carved a reputation as a quick, clever, elusive back. Today, he is Chairman of the ERC, the body that runs the highly successful Heineken Cup competition in European rugby.

'I have two favourite memories from that time. One was my first game for France, for to beat England at Twickenham was very special. Guy Camberabero also played his first game for France in that match. When you are young, only 20 years old, you are on the field and during the game you just play and think of the rugby. It is only before the game and after, that you look at the stadium, you see the people.

1968 was an extraordinary season because halfway through the Championship, we had a game between a French XV and a South-East XV in Grenoble. It was a very bad game for France and after that the selectors changed half the team. But at that time we had many good players, so the selectors could make many changes. We could have had two very good teams. Yet it was still a time when rugby was not that serious in attitude. I was a student and I had my work, so I trained only one or two times a week. I could not spend much time training.

You would say my studies were more important to me then than my rugby although I was pleased and proud to be chosen for France. The southern hemisphere nations were more powerful and we were reminded of that both in 1967 when we played in South Africa and after our Grand Slam in 1968. We went to New Zealand on tour that summer and it was very difficult to play the All Blacks.

When we arrived in South Africa we saw the power of the South African players and it was a wonderful sight, something we had not seen before. They had bigger, more powerful physical players than any country in the northern hemisphere. That was the biggest difference at that time. I played centre and the South African centres were very, very strong. When I ran out and saw the size of them, I thought

Opposite: Lux in full flight against Wales. He was renowned for his excellent ball handling and acute awareness.

Jean-Pierre LUX

to myself, "This is going to be most difficult". We saw the South African team training before the first Test and we thought "Oh, là là!"

But after we lost the first two Tests, we won the third and drew the last so it was a good tour. It was much the same the year after in New Zealand where we lost the three Test matches, although we won in Australia. Those were very hard tours physically. It is never easy to beat New Zealand but it was even harder then because attitudes were different.

In 1970, England came to Stade Colombes in the Championship and we had a wonderful match against them. It was champagne rugby and we won 35-13. I scored one of our six tries that day. Two years later at Colombes, we won 37-12. Again, we scored six tries and I got one of them. That remains a special memory for me, not least because it was the last game France ever played at Colombes.

Recently, I saw a film of that match and it was an extraordinary game, full of running, attacking rugby. Of course, it was a pleasure to play in if you were French. England had some good players, like David Duckham and John Spencer, but they were not a good team.

Of course, there has been a rugby revolution since those times. Therefore, it is not possible to play like that any more because defences are so much tighter now and the physical potential of players is so much better. I still think sides have to try and attack even in today's rugby, but some clubs do not try to play or pass the ball. For me, that is a shame.

It was not really until the 1970s that rugby started to become much more serious in the northern hemisphere. In the Sixties, you still had fun most of the time. But the increasing influence of television and the growing numbers of people who watched the Five Nations Championship matches helped to change attitudes and make people take the game more seriously. It forced changes in preparation, too.

In the 1970s, France changed its style under Jacques Fouroux. Suddenly, you had big forwards dominating the play and it wasn't the same. French rugby changed greatly from the 1960s to the 1970s but the style of the 1970s was a rugby that meant we could win consistently, and winning became more important. Before that, you wanted to win of course but having fun and pleasure was the most important thing.

Opposite: Jean-Pierre Lux touching down against England at Colombes in 1970. France demolished their opponents, winning 35-13.

Colin Meads
New Zealand 1957–71
Lock

Colin Meads made his debut for the All Blacks in 1957 and went on to win 55 caps. Meads was an industrious, fiercely committed lock forward who forged a reputation as one of the toughest forwards ever to play the game.

'New Zealand and South Africa were the strongest teams in the game. But what also made those series so special was that we only used to meet the Springboks every five to six years; that was all.

The great aura of the Springboks meeting the All Blacks that existed in our day has now gone and the reason is they play each other every year these days. That has reduced the importance of it.

I have to say, not being able to win a Test series in South Africa represents one of the real low points of my career. We were right in it in 1960 and 1970 but the fact that we didn't quite do it meant that subsequently we always felt that as a team we had let ourselves down. By contrast, beating South Africa in New Zealand in 1965 was a high but you felt they were always one-up on us and that was a national calamity.

It was very hard to win over there, especially with local referees. There was always this perceived bias and it affected all teams who toured in the southern hemisphere. The only time we had neutral referees was when we went to the northern hemisphere and a Welshman, for example, would referee the England–New Zealand Test match.

But it wasn't just tough playing South Africa – it was hard enough when we went on tour to the northern hemisphere. We would leave in September and play right through to February and by then, the northern hemisphere countries were getting right up for it. They never did the intense training prior to the start of their season – they seemed to play to get fit. But after Christmas they were definitely getting there, which probably explains results like our 0-0 draw with Scotland in Edinburgh in early 1964. And we had a bit of trouble in Ireland on that tour, I seem to recall. They ran us very close, 6-5. As for Wales, they were always one of our biggest enemies on the field. England weren't as strong then as they eventually became in later years.

With the Lions it was different. We sat and waited for them; it was always a big

Colin MEADS

Colin MEADS

thing, there was this sense that "the Lions are coming". A lot of emphasis went into beating them. There was always a big set of trials to sort through our players.

Rugby in New Zealand was intense. If you lost a Test match, it was a tragedy and the country went into mourning. Sometimes that was hard to handle, and you weren't very popular. The taxi drivers the next day would give you stick about being beaten and the players felt it. You felt you represented all those people, the people of your country and rugby was our national game. We put so much emphasis on it.

In 1967, I was sent off against Scotland at Murrayfield. It seemed like a tragedy at the time but as it turned out, because of the huge support I received from the New Zealand public, it seemed to boost my career. When it happened, I feared the worst. You think you will be ostracized, that you'll be thrown out of rugby and have to retire. When it happened, I thought to myself, "That is it, the end of it: it's all over."

Did I go over the top at times in being too physical? I always tell people that anything I ever did on the field I wasn't doing it for personal gain but for the team. If you thought someone was getting an unfair advantage over you perhaps because the referee wasn't pulling him up, you would always say you had to fix it up yourselves. Now, of course, the game has changed so that touch judges help referees and there is an after-match video scrutiny.

But in our time it was a far more rugged confrontation between players. People like myself and Willie John McBride had some huge tussles and there was some violence involved. But out of that came a certain respect. You always had a few beers with your opponents after the game and with people like Willie John, we have been great friends ever since.

There are one or two things I do regret from my career. In 1966 during the Lions' final Test at Eden Park, the Welsh fly-half David Watkins hit me. I went to charge down a kick, missed and as I carried through the little bugger gave me one in the guts. I thought, "You bugger, I'm having you", so I gave him a backhander. I was booed by the crowd for that and I regretted it, I really did. But I had some beers with him that night and it was forgotten between us.

As for the Welsh hooker Jeff Young in 1969, he was warned about continually coming around the line-out onto our side. We kept telling him, do that again and there will be trouble. He took no notice so I hit him. But the end result (his broken jaw) wasn't what I wanted. The thing was, players sorted these things out themselves in those times. We used to say to referees, "You can't see everything, we'll help you."

Opposite: Barbarians' Ian Clarke attempts to tackle New Zealand's Colin Meads.

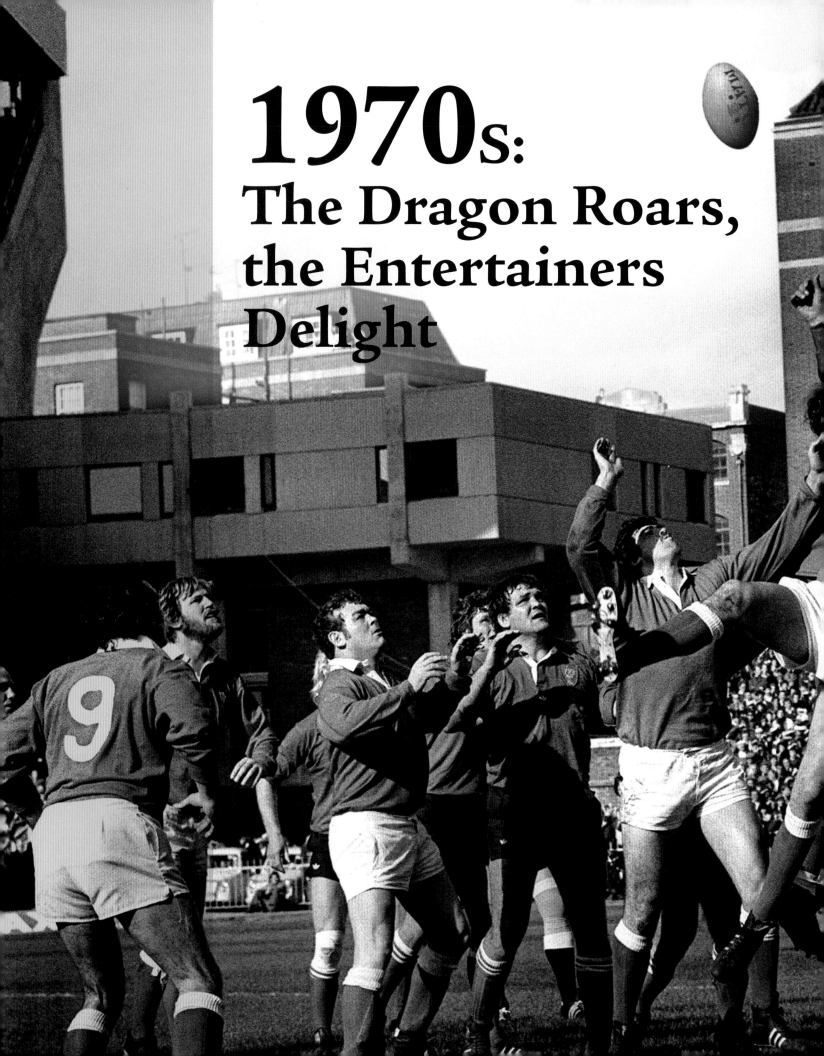

1970s:
The Dragon Roars, the Entertainers Delight

1970s: The Dragon Roars, the Entertainers Delight

If ever an era in rugby football raised hope for the northern hemisphere, it was the 1970s. Fuelled by a unique collection of brilliant, skilful players and a man who was unarguably the most talented, inventive coach in the world at that time and perhaps the finest the game has ever known, the Welsh underpinned a remarkable run of success, not merely for their own country in the Five Nations Championship but on a world stage.

Years of abject failure by the British & Irish Lions in New Zealand and South Africa were suddenly and dramatically overturned. The 1971 Lions achieved what no other visiting Lions team had managed throughout the century: winning a Test series in New Zealand, by two Tests to one with the last drawn.

As if to emphasize this revival was for real, the 1974 Lions then went to South Africa and swamped the Springboks 3-0, again with the final Test drawn. These were achievements unimaginable for the Lions touring teams and if ever rugby in that part of the world seemed on the cusp of sustained success, this was surely the time.

Any Test match won by the Lions in the southern hemisphere was meritorious. But the single defining game of this entire decade was played at Cardiff Arms Park on Saturday, 27 January 1973. It was a match between the Barbarians and New Zealand and it went down in history, rightly so, as probably the greatest game of rugby union ever played. That is some claim, but the style, the invention and the magnificent attacking play of the Barbarians that day merited such a sobriquet. Nor should it be forgotten that the New Zealanders, 17-0 down at one point and weary after a long tour, then responded superbly in similar fashion.

If ever a single game defined and demonstrated what this sport could produce, then that was it. Those who had simply bought tickets expecting to see some kind of decent finale to the New Zealanders' tour, would go to their graves in later years with smiles on their lips. They had been at *the* 'Baa-Baas' game. It was one of the highlights of their lives.

Unarguably, the attacking brilliance, wit and creativity that was behind the Barbarians team's phenomenal play was a derivative from the 1971 Lions in New Zealand. England and Lions wing David Duckham said, 'Some called it the fifth Test match of that tour because the beaten New Zealanders, never having known the bitter experience of losing a Test series to the Lions in their own backyard, had arrived with revenge firmly in mind. We also had a point to prove because some of the media were already beginning to wonder whether the Lions' achievements in 1971 had been a fluke.

> 'The build-up to that match was horrendous ... we were messing about, dropping passes and looking awful. The whole thing was a shambles.'

Previous pages: A line-out battle during the 1978 Five Nations match between Wales and France at Cardiff Arms Park. Wales won the match 16-7 to take the championship Grand Slam.

'Many of the same personnel who had been involved in 1971 were again playing, so perhaps it wasn't surprising it was billed as the fifth Test. One thing was certain – we were determined to show the Lions' achievements had been no fluke.'

As in 1971 a talented side representing the home nations was inspired by the coach of the Lions in New Zealand, Carwyn James. However, to say James's coaching had been the secret behind the Barbarians' triumph would be absurd. As Duckham says: 'The build-up to that match was horrendous and Carwyn was not even there. In training the day before, we were messing about, dropping passes and looking awful. The whole thing was a shambles. It was as well Carwyn wasn't around, he'd have been appalled.

'In fact, his influence was virtually none, on the surface at least. But the Barbarians' committee reluctantly agreed to let him into our dressing room to talk to us for fifteen minutes before kick-off. That was all.

'And, in fact, Carwyn didn't say a great deal. He was almost Churchillian in that regard: he always used his words thoughtfully and sparingly. John Dawes had a similar style, too. But Carwyn did remind us of our responsibilities and he urged us to play the New Zealanders the way we wanted to; in other words, by running the ball and attacking constantly, as we had done in the provincial matches on the Lions 1971 tour. In the Tests, we'd had to be a bit more cautious and pragmatic.

'Carwyn said "Go out and enjoy yourselves but this time we will play them the way we want to play, not the way their style dictates we should." Suddenly, everything from 1971 and that Lions tour seemed to come back. His words were all we needed. Just listening to them made the hackles rise on the back of your neck. We wanted to win for him as well.'

The programme for the 1973 Barbarians v New Zealand game.

Barbarians' Gareth Edwards passes in the 1973 Babarians v All Blacks clash. The match is renowned for Edwards's try, widely regarded as one of the greatest of all time.

James was such a brilliant innovator as a coach, such an inspiration to those who played for him that he convinced the scratch Barbarians side that they could not only win the match but do so with a coruscating demonstration of the game's finest skills. As in 1971, a team inspired by the Welshman, delivered. Magnificently.

Yet they won, 23-11, after a blur of side steps by David Duckham, jinks by Phil Bennett, aggressive running by J. P. R. Williams and ferocious competing by the likes of Fergus Slattery, despite not having three of the key men who had played a huge part in the Lions' triumph eighteen months earlier. Barry John had gone, absurdly early, into retirement, Gerald Davies had pulled a muscle and Mervyn Davies had flu.

There was another disruption, too, before the start. When Gerald Davies withdrew, his fellow Welshman John Bevan was called in. Duckham had been chosen on the left wing, his position for the Lions in 1971 in New Zealand, but Bevan insisted he would only play on the left wing. Thus, Duckham had to switch to the right where, as he said later, 'I had the game of my life. How ironic was that?'

The tries and the manner in which they were scored that day in Cardiff should have lit a whole series of beacons around the British Isles, Ireland and France as to the way forward for the game. Indeed, great conflagrations should have told the world the news; namely, that rugby union played in this style, with this adventure and attacking purpose was the greatest game on the planet, bar none. No rugby stadium would have been big enough to hold the vast throngs who would have sought to get in to see such vivid entertainment.

Not only did a cluster of some of the finest players ever known in British and Irish rugby come together in one era – the likes of Gareth Edwards, Barry John, Gerald Davies, J. P. R. Williams, J. J. Williams, Phil Bennett, John Dawes, Mervyn Davies, Graham Price and a solid nucleus of fine forwards – but the Welsh offered a style, a panache to be envied. They dared to challenge, dared to take risks and they were handsomely rewarded. So, too, were those who went and watched them.

It is no exaggeration to say that these outstanding Welsh players were the main reason the Lions made history in 1971 against the All Blacks. As David Duckham said: 'Two-thirds of the back division was Welsh and a lot of the play was instinctive. Only Mike Gibson of Ireland and myself were not Welsh. So the rest of us just played off them. It was an absolute joy to be in that sort of class.

'Gareth Edwards and Barry John were the major influences on the way we played that 1971 series. You just knew you would get the ball in time and space with them at 9 and 10. Barry was able to stand miles away from trouble because of the length and speed of Gareth's pass. And Barry always decided very quickly what he was going to do. You knew from his body language what he would do, he was that good. But it was having the time and space that made the difference.'

Similarly, Edwards, Bennett, J. P. R. Williams, J. J. Williams and Mervyn Davies were the key men when the Lions went to South Africa three years later and left the South Africans in complete turmoil.

'Only Mike Gibson of Ireland and myself were not Welsh. So the rest of us just played off them. It was an absolute joy to be in that sort of class.'

Opposite: Get out of my way! Gareth Edwards delivers a jolting hand-off to All Blacks fly-half Bob Burgess during the 1971 Lions tour. Even fellow Lion Mike Gibson looks sympathetic to Burgess's plight.

Yet history is always a harsh judge. And the inescapable fact is that, far from leaving a legacy whose influence would last for another decade or more, the great achievements of the 1971 and 1974 Lions were carelessly squandered. In the second half of the Seventies, a Lions touring party set out once again, to New Zealand in 1977. Alas, despite being conquerors up front, they were beaten. It was as though the wondrous achievements in the first half of the 1970s had been no more than an aberration. That was an absolute tragedy, not just for the game in the northern hemisphere but throughout the world.

It could and should have been so different. To win is one thing, but to do so in the style of the team crafted so expertly by Carwyn James ought to have ensured a lasting period of hegemony. But Britain and Ireland's bragging rights were all too brief and there were major reasons for this state of affairs.

The first was that James, the architect of the Lions' greatest triumph in the 1900s, never went on to coach his country. People like James, a maverick character, were always viewed with suspicion by those who sat in power on rugby organizations like the Welsh Rugby Union. He was too unorthodox in his thinking and methods for men of limited potential desperately seeking to protect their own positions of power. Anybody like him was seen as a threat, to be kept out at all costs. Thus, the man who was probably the greatest, most radical-thinking coach British rugby has ever produced, was snubbed in his desire to coach his country. Not just Wales suffered for that – the whole of rugby in the northern hemisphere paid a price.

In an era when the French turned decisively away from their free-flowing backs to the concept of a forward pack of physicality and brutality, it needed someone with James's great vision and imagination to carry on the splendid work he had begun in 1971 and then in 1973 with Llanelli, who beat the touring All Blacks. Alas, under the growing influence of coaches who quickly recognized the simple equation of wins equals extended contracts, rugby in the northern hemisphere countries atrophied. The game became couched in caution, where winning was all that mattered. Of course, James liked winning, but not at the expense of flair,

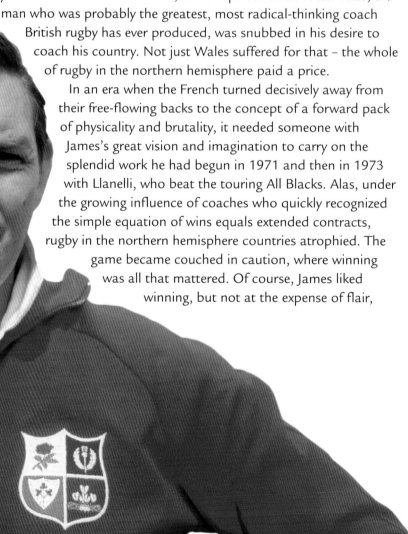

A man apart. Carwyn James was the greatest coach of his era, the best of any era, some said. Being overlooked by his own country for the Welsh national coach said everything about the Welsh committee men of that time.

invention and an attacking creed whenever possible. It was a crying shame and a disaster that his legacy was so rapidly lost.

David Duckham concurred, saying, 'Had Carwyn become the coach of Wales, his influence would have spread everywhere. But the Welsh committee was frightened to death of him. He was years ahead of his time and he rightly pointed out that a single person, the coach, should select the team and take responsibility. That was the way it should have been.

'If he had become Welsh coach he'd have pioneered the way forward for the game, certainly in this part of the world, but maybe around the globe. He would have led the way in steering rugby to embrace movement, speed and skills. That was certainly the way coaching should have gone. Carwyn had a supreme ability to treat players as individuals, not just as a unit. He knew how to bring the best out of individual people, he could pinpoint their strengths and build on them. Yet he never assumed he knew it all and on that 1971 Lions tour he drew heavily on the experience of some of the players.

'His loss to international rugby was crucial to the way the game developed.'

James could have masterminded years of success had he stayed involved at the highest level. But without him, caution crept insidiously into the British and Irish game. Even by 1974, there was a clear diminution in attacking class and strategy outside the scrum. The fact that three of the most creative attacking players in Britain and Ireland – Gerald Davies, David Duckham and Mike Gibson – eventually declined to make themselves available for the Lions tour of South Africa (although Gibson did later travel as a replacement, but only played seven provincial games) was a grievous blow to the potential of the Lions back line. Without them, the Lions three-quarters were functional rather than brilliant. It was their good fortune that they had in Gareth Edwards and Phil Bennett mercurial half-backs, and in wing J. J. Williams a consummate try scorer and finisher of opportunities. Williams had pace to burn and was one of the stars of the tour, finishing with twelve tries, four of them in just two Test matches.

Duckham, in fact, would have given anything to make that tour. He'd missed England's short tour of South Africa in 1972 when he decided a summer's rest was a better idea than travelling halfway across the world. As events would unfold, England's brilliant wing three-quarter, their best attacking back of the decade, would come to regret his decision to stay at home.

But in 1974, he just couldn't make it. 'There was huge pressure on me to go. Alan Thomas, the (late) Lions manager, spoke to me a long time before the tour about going. I hadn't been there and was very keen. But the truth was, I was carrying a nasty groin injury.

'In my day, the only solution to an injury like that was rest or an operation. I decided to rest it. I let it drag on and on, to my own detriment in the end. Because had I known how serious it was and done something about it earlier, I might have perhaps been fit in time for the Lions tour. With hindsight, I might have been able to sort it out and go. But in those days, we were so much more naïve playing as amateurs. In fact, the injury lasted well into the next season.

'It's fair to say that by 1974 the Lions back play was not as convincing as in 1971. There was a better Lions pack of forwards in 1974 but the back play belonged to the 1971 side.'

But in 1977, the Lions' attacking play behind the scrum simply collapsed. The domination of their forwards was such that the All Blacks eventually put only three forwards into their scrum, a hitherto unknown raising of the white flag and humiliation for the once feared and physical New Zealanders.

That should have given the Lions an inevitable platform for victory in the Test series, but their poor three-quarters frittered away so many opportunities that the All Blacks somehow won Tests in Wellington and Dunedin, the Lions succeeding in Christchurch in the second Test. But at Eden Park, Auckland, in the final Test, a fortunate bounce gave New Zealand a try by Lawrie Knight and a 10-9 win that won them the Test series, 3-1. Good judges all over New Zealand were almost too embarrassed to celebrate, so great had been the humiliation heaped on their Test pack. Yet their red faces were nothing compared to those of the Lions forwards who had laid all the foundations for victory, only to see it squandered. The legacy of 1971 was truly gone.

'Things got so bad that if the backs managed to pass the ball all the way down the line without dropping it, it was an achievement.'

As Lions prop Fran Cotton wrote later, 'Things got so bad that if the backs managed to pass the ball all the way down the line without dropping it, it was an achievement.'

British and Irish rugby has often produced outstanding backs of pace, skill and quality. But no decade, either before or since, has seen an emergence in the same era of such world-class talent among the countries of the British Isles and Ireland. Mike Gibson was a genius of a midfield player, a visionary performer and a brilliant reader of the game. True, he lacked one quality – searing pace – but he had just about everything else. Alongside him in the 1971 Lions team was the captain, John Dawes, a superb passer of the ball, intuitive summarizer of the play and a clever tactician. With the likes of wings David Duckham, Gerald Davies and John Bevan around at that time to unleash outside them, Dawes and Gibson were the perfect pair to set up such fast, clever runners.

Then the Lions had probably the greatest half-back partnership a touring Lions party had ever taken abroad. Gareth Edwards and Barry John were geniuses, men of sublime talents. More than that, John proved himself a superb goal kicker in New Zealand in 1971 by contributing 188 points in seventeen games.

John had retired by 1974, driven to quit the game, it was said, by the ludicrous over-hype and fuss that had been created in Wales principally by his exploits for the 1971 Lions and his achievements in a Welsh shirt. John, essentially a private man, couldn't stand the fuss and walked away from the game at the ridiculously early age of 26. His was a grievous loss to the sport in the northern hemisphere. John's brilliant tactical kicking had ended the international career of the New Zealand full-back Fergie McCormack in 1971. But Wales were fortunate: when John retired,

Previous pages: Andy Irvine of the British and Irish Lions in action against South Africa in 1974.

Opposite: Fran Cotton, his face and hair caked with mud catches his breath before a line-out at Athletic Park during the 1977 Lions tour of New Zealand.

Previous pages: Lions room-mates J. J. Williams and Steve Fenwick catch up on the newspaper coverage on the 1977 tour.

Appalling wet weather dogged the 1977 Lions on their tour of New Zealand, but it didn't dampen the crowd's enthusiasm or the competitive nature of the Tests.

up stepped another creative inspiration, Phil Bennett, although in fairness, even Bennett would probably agree he was no Barry John.

But the man who was key to so much achieved by the Lions in the first half of the 1970s and by Wales until 1978 when he finally retired, was Gareth Edwards. The 1977 Lions manager George Burrell made an oblique reference to Edwards by admitting at the end of that losing tour: 'Had one or two players who made themselves unavailable for the trip been on the tour, we would almost certainly have won the Test series.'

That simplistic view overlooked several factors. Firstly, by his own admission, Phil Bennett should probably not have been chosen as captain of that Lions touring party. Secondly, it completely overlooked the crass failings of the Lions backs and thirdly, it was unfair to Edwards. He had slogged his way around South Africa in 1968, New Zealand in 1971 and South Africa again in 1974 on Lions tours. He had more than done his bit. By now married, he wanted to spend some time with his family, which was hardly a heinous crime.

And besides, perhaps Edwards had a suspicion about what might happen on that 1977 tour. He couldn't have foreseen the appalling, wet weather the Lions had to endure for fourteen weeks but he might have suspected there were few

geniuses among the likely Lions backs on the trip. With the greatest respect, players like Gareth Evans, David Burcher, Steve Fenwick, Peter Squires, Elgan Rees, Brynmor Williams and Dougie Morgan were not exactly the equivalent of geniuses like Barry John, Gerald Davies, J. P. R. Williams, David Duckham, Mike Gibson, Gareth Edwards and such like at their peak. Gibson went on the tour but never got into the Test side.

Yet a creative centre like Jim Renwick, of Hawick and Scotland, who could have added so much variety to the Lions three-quarter line in 1977, was overlooked, which has always remained a mystery. David Duckham said 'I would have loved to have gone back to New Zealand with the Lions in 1977 but was out of the England team by then. Clearly, the Lions forwards won their battle but the backs let them down. Conditions were not ideal for backs and it was a very wet tour. But they were the same for both sides.'

They called it the 'Bad News' tour and it most certainly was that. But somehow, it epitomized the shattering of the aura established by the Lions of 1971. It was like a giant balloon that had been suddenly punctured. Belief in their winning ability, simply drained away. Their supremacy in the world game had flowered so splendidly yet been allowed to wither and die cruelly early.

The Way of the Welsh Dragons

The great era of the Welsh set up a magnificent decade of the 1970s for their national team in the old Five Nations Championship. In the ten years from 1970 to 1979, Wales were Champions six times and runners-up on the other four occasions. It was an astonishing tour de force by a nation that was revelling in its prolonged spell in the spotlight. Sustained throughout those years by stalwarts like Gareth Edwards and J. P. R. Williams, Wales established a winning mentality and deep inner belief that drove them to glory time and again. They had the players, both among the forwards and especially in the backs, but most of all, they had the conviction and composure of winners. They knew that most of their opponents in the Championship simply were not in their class.

The belief of many is that it was only France who challenged Wales properly in that time. True, the French gave them some ferocious battles, the Irish, too on occasions. Yet the French were Champions only twice in that era, in 1970 and 1977. Otherwise, only Ireland, in 1974 with their first Championship title since 1951, managed to break the Welsh stranglehold on glory.

What was even more encouraging from a general perspective was that the rugby played by Wales in particular and occasionally France, was spectacular. Intense, highly committed and purposeful, the players sought to expand their game whenever possible. In the latter stages of the decade, the French under the captaincy of little Jacques Fouroux put results and pragmatism before entertainment. But in 1970, for example, the French and Welsh scored twenty tries between them in the Championship. The two countries ended up level at the top of the Championship table, both with three wins and a defeat. But France were deemed winners on point difference.

England, who ended up bottom, threatened the upset of the season when they led Wales 13-3 at Twickenham in 1970, especially when Gareth Edwards went off injured. Alas for the English, a little Welshman named Ray 'Chico' Hopkins took his place and helped mastermind a pulsating comeback to give Wales a 17-13 victory.

The Grand Slam, however, eluded Wales because Ireland finished off what England had started and threatened to do at Twickenham. They led the Welsh 14-0 and, in Syd Millar's final international, held onto that advantage to deny Wales the Slam and the Triple Crown. But only for twelve months.

In 1971, Wales celebrated the opening of their new Cardiff headquarters in appropriate fashion. Their first Grand Slam since 1952 was followed by the Lions, triumph in New Zealand. Remarkably, seven players from the London Welsh club – J.P.R. Williams, John Dawes, Gerald Davies, Mike Roberts, Geoff Evans, Mervyn Davies and John Taylor – went on that historic tour. And the Grand Slam was a thrilling, nail-biting four-match adventure that went to the wire. Tries by Edwards and John set up a narrow 9-5 win over France in Paris, a match of high quality. But the best game of the season was at Murrayfield against Scotland.

The hosts led 18-14 right at the end before Gerald Davies managed to elude

A ticket stub from the 1970 England & Wales v Scotland & Ireland game.

the defence and scoot over wide out on the right. 18-17, with the conversion to come; tens of thousands of Welshmen in the ground could scarcely breathe. It was, too, a mighty tricky one from the far-right side of the field. But John Taylor, left-footed and bearded, stepped up as the coolest man in the ground to slot the kick. They called it the greatest conversion since St Paul and it kept alive Wales's dream with a 19-18 win.

England and Ireland were duly put to the sword, and the talented, multi-skilled Welsh team won their fair reward.

But a year later, trouble flared among old friends. Due to the security situation in Northern Ireland, Scotland and Wales refused to travel to Dublin to fulfil their fixtures. This was unheard of, a gross slight against the Irish and their assurances of safety and security. It was an especially painful blow for Ireland because they had already won both their away games, in France and England, and were eyeing a possible Grand Slam for the first time since 1948.

Years later, that great warrior of an Irish forward Willie John McBride wrote witheringly of that decision by Scotland and Wales. 'Qualities such as strength of character, determination and a willingness to stand up for what you believe in were at the core of what the British & Irish Lions achieved in New Zealand in 1971. Unfortunately, six months later, we in Ireland had seen a complete

The tale of the 1970s. There was always a spare Welshman to out-flank the English defence. Here, full-back J. P. R. Williams is freed by Phil Bennett to expose the fractured English defence.

A golden age for Welsh rugby. This 1972 team photograph taken before Wales's Five Nations clash with England includes J. P. R. Williams (*front-row, far left*), Gareth Edwards (*front-row, second right*) and Barry John (*front-row, third right*). Prop John Lloyd (*with ball*) was captain.

reversal of such qualities by so-called men of rugby football.

'Rugby football had lived through an awful lot in Ireland over the years yet the game had always carried on, whatever the background and however difficult it may have been. Rugby had proved itself bigger than any man of violence for it had conspicuously refused to allow itself to be intimidated by anyone, whatever their views. Imagine our feelings then when we were let down by the ... Scottish and Welsh ... administrations. It was not the players from those countries who were to blame but their governing bodies who claimed that the violence in the North might have repercussions in the South. Those gentlemen who took the decision to abandon their matches with us that year failed Ireland, failed their own countries and failed the game of rugby football.'

Strong words, but then the Irish felt aggrieved at the decision, and no wonder: thoughts of glory had been banished by their so-called 'friends' in the game.

In France, meanwhile, a petit revolution was taking place. The powerful Béziers club started dominating the French Championship in 1971, muscling aside all-comers to lift the heavy 'Bouclier de Brennu' Championship log. Béziers would win the title in 1971, 1972, 1974, 1975, 1977 and 1978. So the national selectors had the bright idea that what worked at club level could be transferred onto the national stage. For the match in Paris against Ireland in 1972, the French chose seven men from Béziers – Jacques Cantoni, Richard Astre, Armand Vaquerin, Jean-Louis Martin, Olivier Saisset, Alain Estève and Yvan Buonomo. Alas, they lost 9-14 and by the last match of the season – Wales's Grand Slam crowning in Cardiff thanks to a 20-6 win over France – the Béziers contingent was down to one.

1973 was a curate's egg of a season. Each country won its two home games but lost twice away, leaving everyone on 4 points. The Scots were said to be winners on points, but such mathematical wizardry hardly constituted a clear Championship success. England, bottom in 1970 and 1972, went to Dublin in 1973, the first country to visit after the boycott by Wales and Scotland the previous year. They were received regally, applauded onto the field at Lansdowne Road with a storm of support.

England lost the match, 18-9, but when their captain John Pullin stood up at the after-match dinner and said simply, 'We may not be much good but at least we turn up!' he brought the house down. Strong, powerfully built men stood up and roared their approval, tears of emotion in their eyes. Rugby football can do this; it can reach the inner parts other games cannot reach.

And, wouldn't you know it, the following year Ireland won their first Championship since 1951, although there was to be no Grand Slam. They did it through just two wins, with a draw and a narrow defeat in Paris (9-6) thrown in.

For the journey to France, the Irish chose a giant of a forward by the name of Moss Keane for his first cap. The former Gaelic footballer played for the Lansdowne club and was as rumbustious as a schoolground mêlée. Trouble was, big Mossie as he was known, was accustomed to a glass or two of Guinness, the black stuff worshipped throughout Ireland. Being physically large, he could handle a few of those with no bother.

'Rugby had proved itself bigger than any man of violence for it had conspicuously refused to allow itself to be intimidated by anyone ...'

What he wasn't so good at was negotiating those squirty little glasses of champagne, which they kept cunningly refilling for you so that you never quite knew how many you'd had. And by midnight after the official post-match banquet in Paris, Moss Keane certainly didn't know how many had been sunk.

Fortunately, help was at hand. His captain for the day, Willie John McBride, had decided to keep a close eye on the new cap and duly found himself with Keane somewhere near the famous Pigalle area of the city. The only problem was, despite having devoured a fine dinner, Keane was still hungry. So McBride parked him against the wall outside a kiosk and went inside for some chips.

But McBride found himself at the end of a long queue and poor Mossie found it hard to wait. Marching into the shop, he spied a sausage on the serving shelf, picked it up and walked out, a contented smile across his chops at the thought of some more food. Alas, what Moss Keane didn't realize was that there were forty-seven other frankfurters attached to the first one, and Keane was leading a trail of them outside onto the pavement, much to the understandable annoyance of the shopkeeper.

But the laughing didn't last long in Paris, nor in any other country of the Championship. On 2 March 1974, England went to Paris to play the French. The weather was foul, early March at its worst and a strike at a British airline had turned Heathrow airport on that Friday night into turmoil.

I remember it well. When you reached the head of the queue, you were asked a simple question by the check-in staff: 'You cannot go on a scheduled flight both ways so do you want to fly scheduled on Air France going out or coming back?'. By complete fortune, I chose the return leg. The decision saved my life.

But you had to take your chances going out. A Saudi Airlines Boeing 707 heading across the Atlantic for Paris, was diverted to London to collect some of the stranded travellers. We took off in shocking weather, bumped our way over the Channel and landed in a blinding snowstorm in Paris. The pilot probably saw the runway about a fraction of a second before his passengers. We banged down hard onto the tarmac and slithered and slid all the way down the runway, for what seemed like ages. Control had disappeared; it appeared simply a matter of luck whether we stopped before the perimeter fence, in the snow and ice. Fortunately, we did, a few feet short, and climbed gratefully out of the aircraft.

England, unusually for them given their hidings in 1970 and 1972 in Paris, put up some proper resistance against France this time. They drew 12-all and could at least hold their heads up that night.

But the journey home the next day was to prove a tragedy for many rugby supporters on the trip. A Turkish Airlines DC10 filled up with stranded passengers in Paris, who had no booking on Air France for the return leg, and headed across the Channel for London. Tragically a door had not been properly sealed prior to take-off and the jet plunged into Ermenonville forest just north of Paris. There was not a single survivor.

Among those who lost their lives were Larry Webb, the former Bedford prop forward of the late 1950s, and Welsh rugby writer Lloyd Lewis. The game mourned its departed: frankly, the rest of the Championship seemed an irrelevance.

1975 saw some distinguished arrivals and departures on rugby's world stage. A young, scruffy-looking French student with long blond hair was given a debut when France went to Twickenham to play England. His name was Jean-Pierre Rives and his orders for the day were simple: 'Go everywhere Andy Ripley goes. Keep beside him, keep tackling him.' Rives did as he was told, France won 27-20 and a legend was born.

So was another when Wales went to Paris to meet the French. Graham Price was a young, promising tighthead prop forward from the Pontypool club and he was given his debut in Paris. So, too, was his fellow club prop, loosehead Tony Faulkner. Some said he was past 30 when he made his debut: 'Big Charlie', as he

Opposite: Moss Keane (*upright*) and Graham Price catch their breath during the 1977 Lions tour.

was known, just smiled and suggested he'd get the job done whatever age he was.

The pair of them joined their Pontypool front-row mate, hooker Bobby Windsor who'd made his debut in 1973 and played the 1974 season so successfully, he'd gone on the Lions tour of South Africa. Thus, the famous, the ever popular Pontypool front row, immortalised in word and song, came together for the delectation of audiences. They were a whole lot more than just three very good rugby players; they were characters. Honed in the tough breeding ground of Welsh club rugby, all three well knew the ins and outs of their trade long before the national selectors came calling. And in Paris came perhaps Graham Price's finest hour.

The French hardly knew what had hit them as tries rained down from all corners of the Parc des Princes. They responded as best they could but when a French attack broke down near the Welsh 25, a visiting boot despatched it upfield. The usual suspects pursued it eagerly, fleet-footed backs with plenty of energy left, for this was late in the game. One other player, however, could be seen making steady, if somewhat ungainly progress in the direction of the ball.

England's Andy Ripley releases the ball as the France forwards pile in to push him into touch.

When neither the closest French or Welsh players could either pick it up or clear it decisively, the other contender came into sight. Graham Price helped it on its way towards the unguarded French line. He got there first and plunged over for the try, Wales's fifth of an extraordinary day, to the famous words of BBC TV commentator Nigel Starmer-Smith, 'They'll never believe it in Pontypool!'

No matter, Pricey was acclaimed for the feat when he got home. Until, that is, he arrived at Pontypool Park on the Monday evening for his regular bout of club training. Pontypool coach Ray Prosser stuck his head around the dressing room door, sniffed haughtily and looking in Price's direction, huffed, 'Pooh, couldn't have been much good as scrummagers them Frenchies, if you 'ad the energy left to run all that way'.

As the likes of Rives, Price, Faulkner and others came into rugby's arrivals hall, so some esteemed names slipped quietly away out of the back door marked departures.

Willie John McBride, Ray McLoughlin and Ken Kennedy all ended their careers after Wales had thumped Ireland 32-4 in Cardiff on the last day of the season. That cost Ireland the Championship, Wales taking it with three wins out of four. The Grand Slam eluded them because Scotland beat them 12-10 at Murrayfield on St David's Day, in a match watched by an estimated 104,000 people.

But the following year Wales went one better, winning another Grand Slam. Not content with hammering Ireland 32-4 in Cardiff the previous year,

'They'll never believe it in Pontypool!'

they then went to Dublin and won 34-9, an unimaginable humiliation for the Irish at Lansdowne Road. In fact, Wales scored heavily all season – 21 points against England, 28 against Scotland and a 19-13 win over France in Cardiff. England lost 30-9 to France in Paris, the French scoring six tries; another example of the foie gras clearly not agreeing with the visitors.

So, in seven seasons of the Five Nations Championship from 1970, England had finished bottom of the table on five occasions. 1976 was their third successive year with the mythical wooden spoon, and they conceded fifteen tries that year alone.

This era was one of complete humiliation for England. David Duckham summed it up succinctly, saying, 'Not untypically, England were in a real mess. I suffered a very nasty hamstring pull in 1976 and lost my place. But quite honestly, I never had the inclination to get back in, things were so shambolic.'

Yet curiously, within the course of just eighteen months early in the Seventies, England somehow beat New Zealand in Auckland, South Africa in Johannesburg and Australia at Twickenham. This trinity of triumphs burst open forever the argument that lightning never strikes twice. It did here, three times. Yet there was no reason to suggest it beforehand and not the slightest cause to think that it would be anything other than a sudden and strange blip, although England also beat South Africa in 1976, 23-6 at Twickenham.

Duckham certainly subscribed to such a view: 'England's fortunes had gone up and down like a yo-yo in those years. So how do you explain those results?

The programme for the 1972 France v England game.

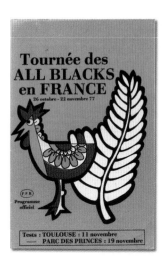

The official programme for the 1977 France v All Blacks game.

'I think we were supposed to go to Argentina in 1973 but that tour was called off and the New Zealanders said, "Come to us." So we did, and I played in that Test match in Auckland. But for us to win it was unheard of, it was a fluke. We were absolute no-hopers for the Test but they clearly thought we'd be easy meat and we just took them on, head-on, ran at them and scored good tries. Jan Webster outplayed Syd Going at scrum-half and John Pullin, the captain, was easily the finest England captain I ever played under.

'So we won it. But there was no sign that England would build on a performance and result like that.'

Likewise when Australia went to Twickenham at the end of that year and were comprehensively beaten, 20 points to 3. Nothing changed in English rugby at that time until a young, ebullient second row forward named Bill Beaumont came on the scene in 1975. Beaumont, with the help of others, would gradually begin to turn England from perpetual losers into a side that not only proved it could win but do so with some conviction and belief.

But before that could happen, Wales and France would end the 1970s as they began it, in dominating style. France won the Grand Slam in 1977 under the Napoleonic-type captaincy of Jacques Fouroux; Wales won in 1978, which proved to be the climax and end of the great careers of Gareth Edwards, Gerald Davies and Phil Bennett.

The 1978 triumph was clinched for Wales with their 16-7 win in the Grand Slam decider against France in Cardiff. At the end of a tough, bruising and unrelenting contest, France's Jean-Pierre Rives embraced Edwards, his old foe, and smiled. 'Gareth, you old fox, you win today. But next year in Paris ... big difference!'

Edwards was so exhausted he could only nod in unconvincing agreement. For the fact was, Gareth Edwards had decided to retire a week or two earlier, as he sat in the dressing room in Ireland after a titanic battle at Lansdowne Road in which Wales had just squeezed home, 20-16. 'I knew then it was time to finish; my body was telling me so,' Edwards revealed later.

The passing of an era can induce a tear or two of emotion, and Gareth Edwards had brilliantly illuminated rugby's stage for twelve long seasons. He'd played all over the world, been acclaimed everywhere for his skills and achieved all a man could achieve in his chosen sport. Including winning a very important little personal contest with Jean-Pierre Rives, one night in Paris.

They'd celebrated long and hard, old friends together after their usual full-blooded contest on the field. And the drinking had carried on far into the Paris night. At some point, Edwards's host, the genial Rives who wasn't used to consuming great amounts of alcohol, decided they should head for another location to continue the evening's celebrations.

Thus, by complete coincidence, three Welsh supporters making their weary way home to their hotel in the small hours were suddenly approached by a Parisian taxi that, without warning, screeched to a halt. The door burst open and out stumbled France's captain who was clearly feeling much the worse for wear. Rives lost his

Opposite: David Duckham making one of his exhilarating runs. Here, he takes on Billy Steele of Scotland.

footing as he fell onto the pavement, almost at the feet of the boys from the valleys.

Concerned at his pal's plight, Edwards quickly stepped out of the taxi himself to help up his friend. At which point, one of the Welsh fans said, 'Well done, Gar. We might 'ave lost the game but we've won the drinking contest, then.'

1979 ended the decade as it had begun, with France and Wales fighting it out for the title. Wales won it again, but their 14-13 loss to the French in Paris meant no Grand Slam. Ireland finished third and bid farewell to the great C. M. H. Gibson.

France's power up front, which had been a feature of these years, was a lesson not lost on England. At last, the 'white tornadoes', as some sarcastic wag had dubbed them, roused themselves and began to discover a pack of forwards in their midst: the likes of Bill Beaumont, Roger Uttley, Fran Cotton, Mike Burton, Nigel Horton and Tony Neary. Their coming together, reflected in England's two wins out of four in 1977 and 1978, was to presage a dramatic revival of English fortunes.

The French had fielded some massive packs during the course of the Seventies. Players like Jean-François Imbernon, Michel Palmié, Robert Paparemborde, Gérard Cholley, Alain Paco, Jean-Claude Skrela, Jean-Luc Joinel, Jean-Pierre Bastiat and others had given the French a steely edge up front that few, apart from the Welsh team, could handle.

Mind you, you had to be careful when you went near those boys, on or off the field. Palmié was subsequently banned from international rugby after he had blinded a player in one eye with a finger, coming through from the

Wales's Gareth Edwards kicks for touch in their 1978 Five Nations match with France.

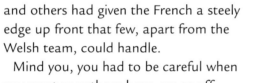

second row of the scrum. Cholley was a former boxer not averse to demonstrating some of his old pugilistic skills and Imbernon, the Perpignan lock, was simply a massive man. He broke his leg in one match at Parc des Princes, and was carried away to hospital. No matter, many hours later, Imbernon returned to his friends' side, his leg encased in plaster. The only problem was that a young English rugby writer was also with the French that night in the darkened nightclub. Honestly, you could hardly see your hand in front of your face. Shapes loomed up in the darkness and disappeared so what the hell hope had you when the 6 ft 6in, 18 stone Jean-François Imbernon stretched his plastered up, broken leg halfway across the room. I felt a sudden impact, followed by a roar of pain from the great bear of a man. You wonder for your own physical safety at such moments.

In general, few northern hemisphere sides could trouble the All Blacks. Scotland lost to them in 1972, 1975 (on an Eden Park pitch that was shin-deep in water after 8 inches of rain had fallen inside 24 hours), 1978 and 1979. England were beaten in 1973, 1978 and 1979, Wales in 1972 and 1978. Ireland succumbed in 1974, 1976 and 1978, but in 1973 they held them 10-10 in Dublin. To this day, it was the closest the Irish have ever come to beating New Zealand. And for those who believe the legend of Munster rugby club was born with the Heineken Cup which they won in 2006, think again. 1978 was Munster's finest day when the mighty New Zealand All Blacks were humbled. It was a day never to be forgotten in Irish rugby history.

But in 1979, six years after the great Barbarians game, there came another spectacular, memorable match in which a northern hemisphere side finally laid its All Blacks bogey to rest.

France had never won a Test match on New Zealand soil and that unhappy trend continued when they went down 23-9 at Christchurch in the first Test of their 1979 tour. They'd already lost two provincial games by that stage, and those familiar Gallic shrugs, which suggest indifference and a wish to be somewhere else, were starting to appear.

But French history is littered with tales of great deeds inspired by special men. Names such as Napoleon, Lafayette, Moulin, Le Clerc and Fouroux are legendary in a variety of French circles and now came another to earn admission to this prestigious elite. Jean-Pierre Rives seemed at times extremely laid back, but when the moment came, he could be the very epitome of inspiration. Thus, the Stade Toulouse flank forward gathered his men about him in readiness for the final match of their tour, the second Test against the All Blacks in Auckland.

The New Zealanders, silly chaps, had arranged the game on a certain date. Clearly, its importance meant nothing to them at the time but to the French, it meant everything. The match was played on 14 July 1979: Bastille Day.

In honour of those brave men and women who had revolted against oppression exactly 190 years earlier, France's rugby men similarly rose up to throw aside years of subjugation. The All Blacks found refreshed opponents confronting them, players who looked twice the performers they had done in the first Test.

In truth, the French touring team had a varying collection of talents. But in forwards like Paparemborde, Dintrans, Joinel and Rives himself, plus some fleet-footed backs who could run like the wind, weave like a fence in a gale and skip as elusively and with the charm of children, France still had plenty to offer. The difference was that Rives, their talisman, their great totem pole, had convinced them this day of French glory could be magnified by a French rugby team making history against the best side in the world. And so it came to pass.

The French attacked from the unlikeliest of situations, scored tries, kicked their goals and won 24-19. History had been made on Bastille Day; all France celebrated. At the heart of the performance had been the extraordinary Rives. That esteemed New Zealand rugby writer Donald Cameron wrote: 'All the time, Rives was hurtling about, setting up the maul here, tackling there, his hair like a beacon for the others to follow.' Rives was that quintessential Frenchman: a touch of laziness, disinterest and nonchalance mixed into one. But when the moment arrived, such torpor vanished, as if a ghostly creation. Then, this human bundle of energy, commitment, desire and dedication would invade the familiar frame. His close friends would often wonder at the paradox of the two characters that seemed to live within the one mind.

> 'All the time, Rives was hurtling about, setting up the maul there, tackling there, his hair like a beacon for others to follow.'

In the southern hemisphere, the spectre of apartheid had become an increasingly unpalatable stain upon the land of South Africa, in most people's minds except the nation's dictatorial white rulers. As the world clamoured with a growing vehemence for the release of Nelson Mandela and his colleagues, so entrenched, frightened men chose not to address the situation. It meant that sporting links with the country were becoming increasingly difficult.

Even in 1974, the British & Irish Lions only departed for their tour against a background of fierce debate and significant protest. One player, the Welsh flanker John Taylor who had been on the 1971 tour of New Zealand, refused to be considered for the tour, a commendable act of courage and conviction that put him several years ahead of most of his colleagues.

The All Blacks could tour the Republic but the Springboks did not visit New Zealand once during the 1970s. They hadn't been there since 1965 and apart from their ill-fated tour in 1981, they wouldn't go again until 1994.

Thus, just two Test series were played in that time between the world's greatest rugby-playing nations. Those tours by New Zealand, in 1970 and 1976, both resulted in 3-1 Test series wins for the South Africans. Yet the outcome of both had been in doubt at kick-off in the final Test of both series. In each case, Ellis Park, Johannesburg witnessed some extraordinary dramas. In 1970, South Africa, 2-1 up in the series, sneaked home 20-17 and six years later, with the Springboks holding an identical lead after winning the third Test, they managed an even tighter victory, 15-14, in the last Test.

A commemorative brochure for the 1970 All Blacks tour of South Africa.

ALL BLACKS
IN
S.A.

1970

An Official Publication   25c   N. Ampelific Publicans

Both series were fine contests, yet the shadow caused by South Africa's repugnant white regime hung over the occasions. As other sports isolated South Africa for its stand, rugby dragged its feet, studied its navel and did next to nothing. As it has done too often in its long life.

Of course, events of the 1980s would change all that, for all time. But what few had foreseen was that a third southern hemisphere rugby-playing nation would seize the limelight in the next decade. Even the two traditional powers in that part of the world would be forced to look to their laurels as that young, vibrant nation strode with typical confidence onto the world rugby stage.

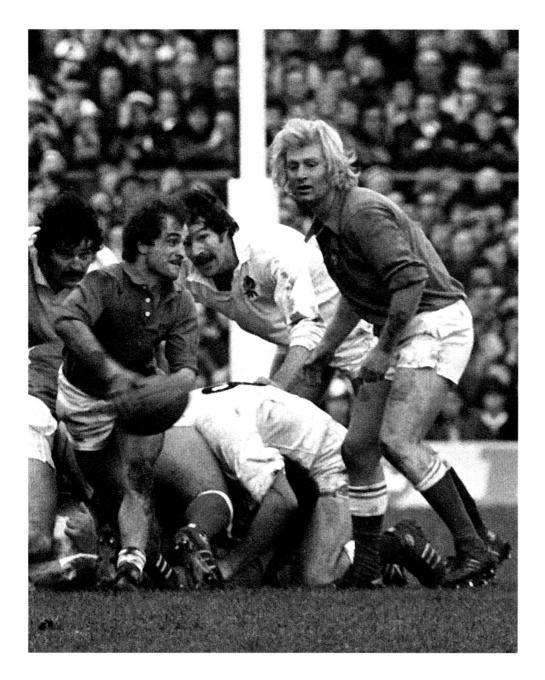

Two of the greatest characters French rugby has ever known: The late and inimitable Jacques Fouroux (*left*) passes the ball watched by the great Jean Pierre Rives in a match against England at Twickenham.

Jean-Pierre Rives

France 1975–84

Flanker

He became a legend in French sport, revered by his countrymen for his deep love of the game and friendships rugby afforded. He was not big but as brave as a lion, a point proved when he played a Test match against Australia in 1981 with a dislocated shoulder. Representing Stade Toulouse and then Racing Club, Paris, he won 59 caps for France between 1975 and 1984 and led his country on thirty-four occasions.

' When I look back and reflect on my career, it is as though everything was a dream. It was a fantastic, magic time of my life. The people in rugby were wonderful, the players I met became friends. It was incredible. Then one day you wake up and think, "This must have been a dream."

My life was not planned to become a rugby player. I was watching television one day and saw a match and decided I wanted to play this game. It began from there, in very simple circumstances.

I enjoyed everything so much about the game: those were truly special times. Jo Maso and Walter Spanghero, two of France's greatest ever players, were my heroes when I was young. Then, one day, I played with them. Can you imagine the pleasure that gave me?

All the players in that era were really lucky because we had so much fun together. Sure, there was not money like today but money cannot buy those friendships. We enjoyed each other's company through rugby, we met all types of people in the game and saw countries all over the world. That is a great opportunity in your life.

Never forget the value of friendships. Rugby was the story of a ball with some men. But when the ball disappears the men are still there and that is the story of humanity, friendship and brotherhood.

But some things have changed. French rugby was a big mess at that time. We never knew what we were doing and that was why we were dangerous. We were

Opposite: Jean-Pierre Rives. A human bundle of energy, skill, desire and dedication.

never predictable and teams did not know what to expect from France.
I remember my great friend Serge Blanco. Nobody knew where he was going on a field, even himself. Nobody knew what he would do next. It was just a game, a very special game, but we played it with our friends to have fun together.

The game gave us great friendships but also great bruises! There were some very tough matches, especially in the French Championship. For the first 15–20 minutes of every match you tried to stay on your feet. You didn't want to go on the floor; it could be very dangerous.

Most of the rules were controlled by the players on the field. I don't know if that was good or not. But it was a game of contact and yes, sometimes a game of fighting. But I feared if you put out the fight you took away a lot of the passion.

In that time, you had your opponent and he would be there for the full eighty minutes. That was the time you knew you had to battle him. Sometimes it took you seventy minutes to win that little war against him. But now, players start a match, they try to intimidate an opponent and then they are gone by half-time or just after. Then a new player comes on.

There was a very special relationship between the French and Welsh players at that time. We had some hard matches against Wales, very hard. But there was respect, too. Players like Gareth Edwards became friends, and they still are.

Rugby has become cleaner, that is certain. But it has lost much of the drama it always had and I regret that. It is now a modern sport with no more fighting, no more wars between teams. Totally different. The fighting of the French forwards has ended but maybe they have killed the dream, too. Now, everything is neat, everything is planned. But the French are not very good at this because we follow our hearts as people. We are good when we do unexpected things. I like that.

I enjoyed the game when the outcome was unclear and the method was unknown to anyone. I don't want a pre-arranged match.

I confess, I do not like some of the modern rules. The one that allows players to hide the ball from opponents (the rolling maul) and stay in the middle of a group of players just edging forward a yard or two at a time is absurd. You are not allowed to tackle these players because you concede a penalty. But if you are not allowed to tackle, you don't have real rugby any more and that is stupid.

Keeping the ball among the forwards in that method is not exciting, just boring. It also means players do not pass the ball freely. But rugby is surely about passing the ball. It is about magic so that when you see a game with a lot of passes, it is exciting.

In my view, we have to change the rules before the rules change the game forever, change the people and their minds. Players today are very good, very fit and very clever. It could be fantastic again. But we need to free the game from these bad rules. We need to return to a game where the guy with the ball is in charge. He should have to pass the ball to keep it alive. Otherwise, a player just keeps the ball, takes a tackle, the ball takes forever to come back and it is boring.

The All Blacks are still playing in their usual way. They play very well but they play like they did. However, other countries have changed too much.

I still love rugby but perhaps most of all, my idea and my memories of it. If you are lucky, you can play this game at any time and it is a dream, a special game. I was lucky to play at a fantastic period of time and we had incredible lives. People say friendships are no more in rugby but I don't accept that. I am sure that in twenty years time this generation of players will be saying the same thing. That is the magic of rugby.

Jean-Pierre Rives demonstrates his strength and flair as he breaks through the English lines.

Gareth Edwards
Wales 1967–78
Scrum-half

Gareth Edwards became the most famous player of his time. Strong, quick, skilful and fiercely determined, he forged memorable half-back partnerships with Barry John and Phil Bennett that lit up Welsh and British and Irish Lions teams of his era. He still holds the Welsh record for the most consecutive Tests, all fifty-three from 1967 to 1978.

What is most satisfying to me now when I look back on my career is the pleasure that other people seem to have had out of it. Their comments about those days and the matches we played for the Welsh or the Lions are a wonderful reminder of what was a very special time for all of us.

We thoroughly enjoyed ourselves playing sport. Welsh rugby was at its dominant best and I think people today can stand back and say "Yes, those were good times for rugby and for Wales." There seems to be no let up in the enjoyment people take from those memories. And I don't mean just the Welsh, but the Irish, English and Scots, too. What the Lions did in those years was special.

But I don't look back and think of it as, 'We were this or that'. It was just that we were young, we were playing to win and for the pure enjoyment. It wasn't your career, it was a release from work. And it wasn't just an enjoyable period of time but a successful one, too.

If you asked me what has best stood the test of time I'd say the friendships, the camaraderie we achieved out of it all. I still remember the good matches and whether we won or lost, but mind you, the disappointment of defeats lasted a lot longer than the wins.

When you analyse those times, I certainly think it's fair comment to say that attitudes changed from 1968 to 1971. In fact, they did so dramatically. People were far more aware of what was going on by then and remember, too, the law preventing kicking directly into touch except inside the 25, had helped open up the game enormously. It became very attractive, but there was also a greater emphasis on winning among the northern hemisphere countries.

Opposite: Edwards's was Wales's youngest ever captain, leading his country at the age of 20 against Scotland in 1968. He also possessed some hidden talents, such as the ability to do standing backward somersaults and once eating fourteen steaks in one sitting.

Gareth Edwards

The Olympic ideal is chiefly to take part but winning was always very much the focal point in the southern hemisphere. By the end of the 1960s and after those three successive losing Lions Test series people were starting to say, why do we send good players but don't win? That led to a different attitude by the administrators and players from future generations. We had been a team full of great individuals that never played as a team. But after 1968 we began to take things much more seriously. We had taken notice of the southern hemisphere approach.

The 1971 tour created such a stir because the Lions won. We had a very good coach (Carwyn James), a man who understood and read the game. He was a great man manager, too, and wasn't afraid to ask his senior players how to succeed and learn from their experience.

People have often asked me why the northern hemisphere didn't maintain the supremacy it established over the southern hemisphere in the first half of the 1970s. Well, we became stronger in the forwards, our scrummaging was stronger than theirs. So we tended to adapt and change and put a greater focus on that. In 1971, we only got 30–40 per cent of the ball and played an adventurous style because we could never control the game up front. We weren't in charge in the forwards.

But in 1974 because we were so much in charge up front, the logic was, rightly or wrongly, when we won the ball we would use it but not give it away. I remember saying, if we use all this ball, they will bash us down and seize the loose ball. So we had to be a little more careful and probably didn't have the cavalier attitude and approach of 1971. So I suppose there wasn't the same sense of adventure.

In 1977, the Lions were within a whisker of winning the series until that last-minute debacle. As for George Burrell (Lions manager) saying they'd have won the series if a couple of leading players had made the tour, well, I don't know to whom he was referring. But if one of them was myself then I take that as a compliment.

Perhaps what some people don't know is that the Lions tried to get me out to New Zealand for the final week of that tour. They had injuries and wanted me to go. But I had done no preparation at all. And my original reason for not going wasn't a rugby decision.

What people forget in today's professional game is that we held down jobs then. But for the generosity of our employers, we wouldn't have been able to play the amateur game at that level. My boss paid for me to go to South Africa twice and New Zealand once on Lions tours. In 1977, I felt I just couldn't ask again, it wouldn't have been fair. Also, I was married with a young family and I felt my family was more important to me by then than another rugby tour. I'd been there before and done it all.

And I've never regretted not going in 1977. I often think, what if I had? But I always come back to my original decision and that itself is testimony to having made the right decision in the first place.

My overall memories of that time? I feel so fortunate to have experienced all that. What you realize in sport is that there's a very fine dividing line between success and failure. We were not only fortunate in Wales and with the Lions to enjoy success but we played in an era where there was a certain style of rugby. And no one should think the exciting young players who strode the stage at that time only came from Wales. That isn't true. Look at the likes of David Duckham in England, Mike Gibson and Fergus Slattery in Ireland, Andy Irvine in Scotland. It was a very exciting era all round and I'll always feel grateful for the opportunity and good fortune to have been a part of it.

During Gareth Edwards's era the Welsh side dominated the Five Nations Championship, winning the title seven times, including three Grand Slams.

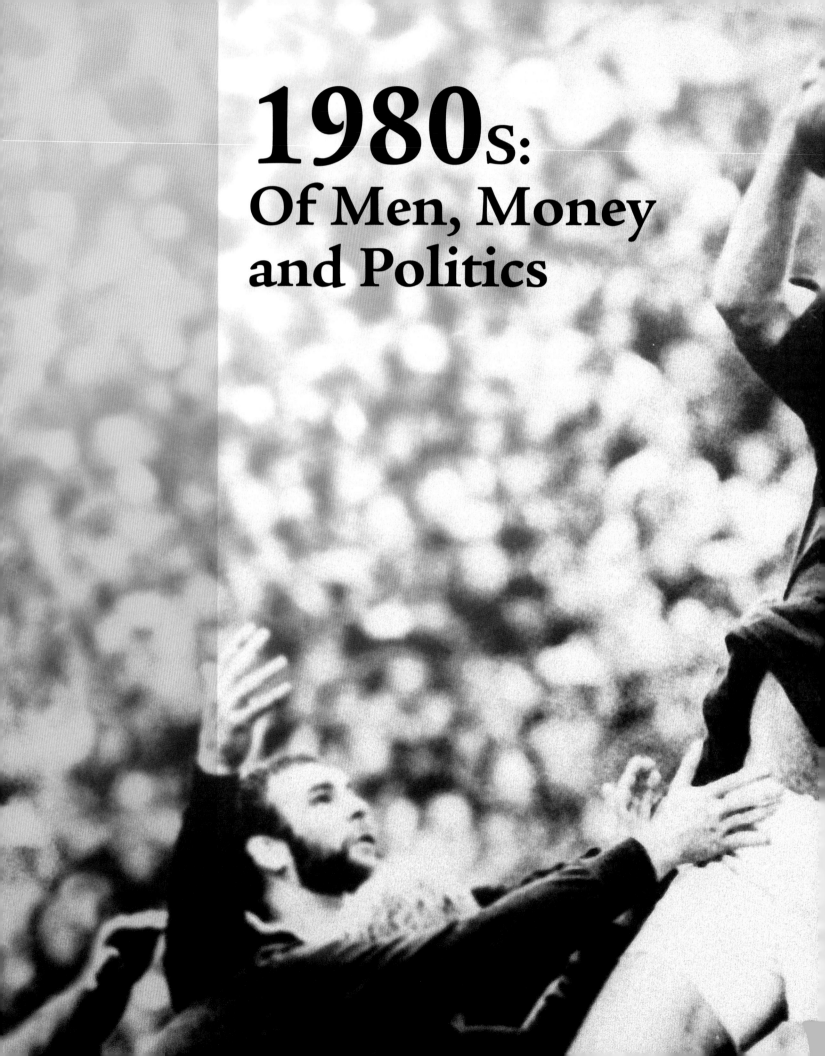

1980s:
Of Men, Money and Politics

1980s: Of Men, Money and Politics

Australia had been playing the British Isles and Ireland since 1899, France since 1928, South Africa since 1933 and New Zealand since 1903. So you could hardly say Australian rugby arrived in the 1980s.

Mind you, of the sixty-eight Test matches they'd contested with New Zealand from 1903 to 1979, the Australians had won just fifteen against the All Blacks' forty-nine. But it would be crass to ignore the Aussie boys of 1949 for their dramatic series win over the All Blacks in New Zealand.

Nevertheless, the 1980s was the decade when the Wallabies took the rugby world by storm. And some storm it was. They kicked off the era in fine style, winning a Test series at home against New Zealand for the first time since 1934. A record crowd for a rugby union game in Australia, some 48,698, poured into the Sydney Cricket Ground to see the All Blacks beaten 26-10, a result that gave the Wallabies the series by two Tests to one. That success set up a barnstorming period for Australian rugby in which they captivated the world with their stylish, innovative play and gave all manner of problems to their opponents. Frankly, their rugby was like a breath of fresh air.

As with the Welsh in the Seventies, a uniquely talented collection of players came together to lift Australian rugby to the peak of the world game. The names of the finest have been well documented: Mark Ella, David Campese, Andrew Slack, Roger Gould, Steve Tuynman, Andy McIntyre, Simon Poidevin, Paul McLean, Tom Lawton, Nick Farr-Jones, Michael Lynagh, Michael Hawker, Steve Williams, Steve Cutler, 'Topo' Rodriguez and more.

'Just a few minutes listening to him and you'd want to lace up your boots, put your kit on and get onto the field. He was incredibly motivating.'

But Australia brought something else to the party, a factor that was uniquely their own. In coaches like Bob Templeton, Bob Dwyer and Alec Evans, they had men of rugby steeped in knowledge of the game. And in the mercurial, unconventional Alan Jones they had a true professional and motivator par excellence, a man of wisdom and cunning who could probably have lifted people out of the cemetery with his powers of oratory. The England fly-half of the Eighties, Rob Andrew, spent a season in Sydney club rugby and talked often with Jones. 'Just a few minutes listening to him and you'd want to lace up your boots, put your kit on and get onto the field,' Andrew said later. 'He was incredibly motivating.'

These men urged, cajoled and inspired Australian rugby to its finest era. Within eleven years, Australia would banish humiliating memories of being lightweight opposition, a country where the British & Irish Lions could stop off en route to New Zealand and play a couple of gentler, warm-up Test matches before the real business end of the tour began across the Tasman Sea in New Zealand. More than

Previous pages: Springbok Hennie Bekker, jumping with the ball, gets a lift from team-mate Okkie Oosthuizen and Burger Geldenhuys during the controversial third Test at Eden Park in September 1981 against New Zealand.

Opposite: Australia's Mark Ella hands the ball off as he is tackled.

that, they would bedazzle and enchant the tough New Zealanders with a wonderful attacking brand of rugby forged on a cluster of kids; win their first ever Grand Slam on a tour of the Britain and Ireland; become only the second Wallaby side in history to win a Test series in New Zealand; and then cap it all by winning the Rugby World Cup in 1991.

As with all things in life, the Australians did all this in their own way, with their unique approach. One commodity seldom in short supply in Australia is self-confidence; it is a trait that seems to originate from birth. These people have a deep-seated belief that they can beat anyone, at anything, at any given time anywhere in the world. Nor is that froth, a false front that masks deep misgivings and fears. Australians did more than enough in two World Wars to prove that point to anyone. Their familiar taunting of imminent rivals can weary some, but their optimism is infectious and it reveals a very special people, human beings ever anxious to achieve, to get on and make progress in all walks of life.

Fear never stalks them; it is a foe uncommon to these folk. Where the people of other nations of the world can be conservative, cautious and bound by convention and tradition, the Australians simply love to buck a trend, to engage in a challenge where the odds are stacked against them. They have neither fear in such circumstances nor the tiniest doubt that they will prevail. And frequently they do. Of course, the weather conditions in Australia and generally firm grounds lend a decided advantage to rugby players who seek the ball in their hands and a good surface on which to run, side-step and swerve. Thick mud more akin to the farmyard tends to have a negative effect on such activities.

Thus, the defining era of Australia's rise from eager rugby competitors to a nation feared by every other in the world began in 1982. As so often with Australians, it happened against a background of great adversity.

Firstly, it is essential to understand the tribal nature of the in-fighting that exists between those who represent the two great rugby-playing states of the country's eastern seaboard: Queensland and New South Wales. Alley cats rarely scrap with the intensity of these two.

A coach selected for the national job from either state is guaranteed to receive the adulation of his own state and the utter vitriol of the other. The notion of pulling together and backing the man whatever his origins is anathema to many.

Thus, when the incumbent, Queensland's Bob Templeton, was voted out of office (following the Wallabies' loss of three out of four Tests on their 1981 tour of Britain and Ireland under him) and Sydney's Bob Dwyer was appointed, a storm worthy of the higher digits on the Richter scale broke over Australian rugby. Even worse, Dwyer then disregarded Queensland's 41-7 thumping of New South Wales and the state's 18-7 win over the touring Scotland team, results masterminded by two outstanding players, Roger Gould and Paul McLean. For the first Test against the Scots, Dwyer bravely left both Queenslanders on the bench, opting instead for two of the brilliant Sydney-based Ella brothers, Mark at fly-half and Glen at full-back. He did it, perfectly aware that the Test match would be played in the Queenslanders' lair, Ballymore. You certainly couldn't accuse Dwyer of dodging a difficult issue or lacking bottle.

But then this remarkable man had never shirked a challenge in his life.

Even Dwyer had to swallow hard when the Scots took the Test, 12-7, their first ever Test match win over a major rugby-playing nation in the southern hemisphere. The newsprint was still sizzling when it reached the streets in Brisbane. And even Dwyer had to concede the experiment had not worked, for the Ellas were dropped and the two Queenslanders, Gould and McLean, reinstated for the second Test. The result? A 33-9 trouncing by Australia which earned a 1-1 draw in the series.

This new era of Australian rugby was going to be different, whatever else it was.

No sooner had the dust settled on this opening spat, than the real storm broke. The Wallabies were due to make a fourteen-match tour of New Zealand but ten Test players, nine of them from Queensland including McLean, made themselves unavailable, pleading work commitments. Some read into it the obvious, that the Queenslanders didn't fancy getting their backsides kicked all around New Zealand, by not just the locals but their own Sydney-based coach. But whatever the truth, Bob Dwyer faced a crisis and he solved it in the way he has sorted out problems all his life: namely, by confronting them head-on.

Australia flew over the Tasman Sea with one of the most inexperienced international squads that has ever toured. They chose all three Ella brothers, Glen and Mark aged 23 plus Gary, 22, a 19-year-old wing from the ACT. Most people had never heard of named David Campese, the 22-year-old centre, Michael Hawker and 22-year-old first five-eighth, Tim Lane. The half-backs were 24-year-old Phillip Cox and Dominic Vaughan, two years younger.

'The team aroused extraordinary affection and commanded a universal respect.'

Even up front, the kindergarten ranks were just as profuse. Steve Tuynman (19), Simon Poidevin, Steve Williams and Ross Reynolds (all 23), Steve Cutler and Shane Nightingale, both 22. This selection flouted all the conventional laws of the game. You didn't go out in the dark onto your local park with so many kids around you, never mind take them to New Zealand for a hard tour against the All Blacks. This was, many said, simply another illustration of Dwyer's zany approach.

Judgement is best left in the hands of the most astute, the impartial observers. So the words of that great New Zealand rugby writer Terry McLean serve best to sum up what Dwyer and his babes achieved during the seven and a half weeks they spent on that tour. McLean wrote: 'It would not be possible to compute the number of converts Mark Ella's salvation army band had attracted by the end of the tour. Sufficient to say that by playing, constantly, a game of the style desired by their coach Bob Dwyer ... the team aroused an extraordinary affection and commanded a universal respect. It would not be too much to say that this was the most significant Wallaby team which has ever toured New Zealand. The good that it did to Kiwi rugby was beyond the comprehension of the classiest computer IBM has ever made'.

All this, mark you, despite the fact that the Wallabies lost the Test series 2-1. But with their glorious upset win over the All Blacks by 19-16 in the second Test at Wellington, these Australians confirmed themselves as supreme demonstrators of the game's finest skills. It was a performance of singular genius and it set the seal for a decade of Australian invention and rugby entertainment, despite their loss of the series decider in Auckland, by 33 points to 18.

The great irony that subsequently overtook Australian rugby was that while so many of those brilliant young players survived what everyone assumed would be a harrowing ordeal, Dwyer, the man whose courage and bravery had masterminded their attacking philosophy, did not.

A challenge to him as national coach, not from a Queenslander but another Sydney-based coach Alan Jones, unexpectedly succeeded and Jones took the reins. His was to be a very different regime.

Jones's and Dwyer's characteristics and approach to coaching could not be more dissimilar. Jones, Oxford University educated, became a speech writer for an Australian prime minister. A man of formidable educational intellect, erudite and savvy as well as being a master of psychology, Jones took the Wallabies on their 1984 tour of Britain and Ireland and, reaping the benefits of Dwyer's bold selection policy that had seen players like the Ellas, Campese, Poidevin, Williams and Cutler emerge, added his own unique element to the mix and introduced still more young, hitherto unknown players. Both men knew what they wanted from their teams but Jones's was a more rigid approach in which players were made to understand and acknowledge to a far greater degree their own responsibilities and the opportunity being laid before them. His man-management skills were considerable.

'The Gucci effect, mate; long after you've paid the price, you remember the quality.'

Dwyer was much more laid back, a natural and easy communicator who understood the game deeply. He might have lacked Jones's often brilliant turns of phrase – 'It's the Gucci effect, mate; long after you've paid the price, you remember the quality'– but he was a shrewd, clever tactician and he believed in giving his players freedom and responsibility.

Jones's Wallabies lost a 1984 series to New Zealand in Australia, by two Tests to one. They won the first Test and led 12-0 in the second, yet somehow allowed a glorious opportunity to slip through their fingers. The All Blacks, coached by the wily Bryce Rope, got a narrow 19-15 win in the second Test and then squeezed out the third, 25-24, at the Sydney Cricket Ground.

Later that year, the Wallabies landed at London's Heathrow airport on a golden, early autumn October morning and Jones took the place by storm. Most British rugby writers had never experienced a rugby coach like this. Immaculately attired (as he expected his players always to be), Jones handled the opening press conference with aplomb. It proved to be a tour that matched the billing.

With a brand of rugby that delighted the vast crowds that saw them at every opportunity, the Wallabies moved serenely to their first ever Grand Slam triumph on a British and Irish tour. They did it with a style and élan to be envied, perfecting loop passes and mis-moves that regularly confounded defences. Young men accepted the opportunity presented to them and fulfilled their potential. Andrew Slack's calm, intuitive reading of the play was a valuable foil to the exciting, off-the-cuff skills of Mark Ella and David Campese. Roger Gould was a colossus behind them at full-back, his long raking kicks both relieving pressure and launching attacking positions. Farr-Jones's youthful exuberance, quality passing, sniping around the fringes and general intelligence set up this back line, in which wing Brendan Moon was unlucky to break his arm at Twickenham.

But Australia had a whole lot more than just a glitzy set of backs. In Andy McIntyre, Tom Lawton and Topo Rodriguez, there was a front row of might and technical excellence. Steve Williams and Steve Cutler were powerful, ball-winning locks in the second row and a back row of Simon Poidevin, Steve Tuynman and David Codey let no one down. The pushover try the Wallabies inflicted on the Welsh in Cardiff was somehow symbolic of Australia's phoenix-like rise, combined with Wales's decline since the end of their glory era.

Cleverly, Alan Jones had earmarked Steve Cutler as his No. 1 line-out jumper a year earlier. Approaching him after a Sydney club match one afternoon, Jones took the lock forward aside and told him, 'Get yourself properly fit and in form. You're

Australia's Michael Lynagh in action against Ireland in their 1984 tour of Britain and Ireland. The Wallabies introduced a fresh style of rugby, which not only thrilled the crowds but also led them to their first Grand Slam of the British Isles and Ireland.

going to be my top line-out man on the British and Irish tour in 1984.'

But more than all that, the Australians were courteous, friendly, happy tourists whom the British and Irish supporters took to their hearts. They were outstanding ambassadors for their country. Led by the quiet but dignified Andrew Slack, they won legions of fans in beating England 19-3, Ireland 16-9, Wales 28-9 and Scotland 37-12. The Barbarians were then seen off 37-30 in a typically rousing end-of-tour finale.

Following Dwyer's tradition, Jones introduced some notable young talents not just to his squad, but his Test team. Chief among these were a young scrum-half named Nick Farr-Jones and a baby-faced young centre by the name of Michael Lynagh. Both would become not just future Wallaby captains but household names in the game the world over by the time their careers ended. The fact that Lynagh, most uncharacteristically, missed six goal kicks in the England match, revealed the chasm between the two teams.

In a sense, the groundwork had been prepared for these marvellously entertaining Wallaby sides by an outstanding Australian Schools side that toured Britain and Ireland in the late 1970s. With the three Ella brothers at the helm, they proved so strong a draw that thousands went to Twickenham to see their match against England, even though thick fog meant it was impossible to see even halfway across the field.

David Campese looks around for support as he drives forward.

Jones's success on the 1984 tour meant he was still in the job in 1986 when Australia went back to New Zealand for a three-match Test series. The fall-out from an unofficial tour to South Africa by several leading All Blacks meant a new, younger New Zealand side confronted them for the first Test. They called them 'the Baby Blacks' but they still managed to reverse the Wallabies 13-12 first Test win, with an identical score in the second Test at Dunedin.

That night somehow epitomized the many and varying characters within the Australian team. David Campese came off the field, allegedly to endure a berating from his coach, after dropping one high kick. 'I told the world you were the Bradman of rugby; you've let me down,' Jones is said to have snapped at his brilliant three-quarter.

The Australian bus from the Carisbrook ground back to their basic city hotel was cast in silence and gloom. Campese wasn't feeling a whole lot more cheerful later in the evening, when he should have been at the official dinner. Instead, I looked up from my book in the hotel dining room to see a familiar face peering down. 'Mind if I join you?' asked Campese. It was the start of a great friendship.

Campese talked long and hard, about all manner of things. Always a sensitive man, he'd found Jones's words tough but, worse still, he was struggling to accept the modesty of his own performance that day. But with rugby, there is always another game ahead.

Thus, in the early hours of that Sunday morning, an extraordinary scene unfolded in the lounge of the team's hotel. A large throng of players surrounded a miniature greyhound track over which Master of Ceremonies Nick Farr-Jones presided. The dice was thrown, a player could move his counter forward accordingly down the course. As the winning post came close, the excitement grew. The Wallabies had, temporarily, forgotten their woes and it was essential therapy.

The deciding Test was at Auckland and Australia, back to their best even against a strengthened New Zealand side containing all its (briefly) banned players, were comfortable winners at 22-9. It was the climax of a magnificent six years for Australian rugby, a short period of time that had seen them climb the ladder of world rankings with the dexterity of a Victorian lad shinning up a chimney.

The official programme for the 1984 Barbarians v Australia game.

The Outsiders

Australia's emergence as a real power in world rugby coincided with the sad decline of South Africa. The 1980s was to see the Springbok emblem increasingly tarnished, dragged down from its once proud perch by its government's intransigence at the world's growing revulsion at the apartheid system.

Trouble had started as early as 1969/70 when South Africa toured Britain and Ireland. The threat of protests forced the opening match of the tour against Oxford University to be switched from the university ground at Iffley Road to Twickenham where, it was thought, security would be easier. Maybe it was, but only thanks to draconian rules that saw three sides of the stadium closed off, with spectators corralled into the west stand. Four hundred policemen were on duty inside the ground where the more militant protestors had gathered. Outside, a silent protest against the evils of apartheid was supported peacefully by thousands of ordinary people.

The match was played against a cacophony of whistles, blown by the protestors. Two demonstrators succeeded in getting onto the ground at half-time but to little avail. But if the policing was easier at Twickenham, winning wasn't for the stunned, distracted Springbok players. They went down 6-3 to Oxford University, a result that foretold considerable difficulties ahead on the tour.

In the event, Dawie de Villiers' poor side did not win a single Test match on the trip. They went down 6-3 to Scotland and 11-8 to England, managing draws in

A brochure for the controversial 1981 Springboks tour to New Zealand.

Opposite: In one of the darkest days in rugby history, a light aircraft dive-bombs the field during the third Test between New Zealand and South Africa at Eden Park in 1981. In other fly-pasts, flour bombs were dropped as part of the protest against the 1981 Springboks tour of New Zealand, one of which injured an All Black player.

Ireland and Wales. Overall, they lost five and drew another four of their twenty-four matches, a record of unimaginable modesty for the pride of South Africa.

Not without good cause were the rugby authorities of the British Isles and Ireland known for their dinosaurial traits. They had insisted the tour should go ahead, but it did so only with great difficulty and in circumstances that reflected poorly on the game. When it was finally over, those in senior office were prodded to see sense at last by their government. It would be twenty-three long years before South Africa appeared at Twickenham again, twenty-four years before they went to Cardiff, twenty-five years before they visited Murrayfield and twenty-eight years before they returned to Lansdowne Road.

In fact, South Africa were wanted hardly anywhere. The Australians didn't see them from 1971 until 1993 and most countries of the world felt likewise. However, to their shame, countries like England, New Zealand, France, Ireland, the 1980 British & Irish Lions and the 1986 New Zealand Cavaliers, the latter little more than an allegedly money-making outfit, scuttled off furtively to the Republic in a selfish gesture that said as much about them as their desperate hosts. So, too, did a South American combined team, playing them in the Republic in 1980, 1982 and 1984 and inviting them back, to those renowned world rugby venues of Montevideo, the Uruguayan capital, and Santiago, in Chile, for two games. That South African rugby had come to this, an increasingly desperate trawl around the world to find anyone still prepared to play them, said everything about the plight to which their brutal government had subjected them.

There was one exception to the rule, where an overseas country still wanted the representatives of the white apartheid government in their midst. In 1981, New Zealand's blinkered rugby officials decreed that the South Africans were welcome to tour their country.

Rugby observers in the northern hemisphere who had ever taken the trouble to look out of their own backyard and, more especially, travel to other parts of the world, shook their heads in amazement when the New Zealand RU announced the tour would go ahead. They thought they had a pretty good idea of what would happen and it duly did. To this day, some of the scars remain sore.

If you were happy watching a rugby match from behind a barrier of barbed wire or looking on as some 3,000 protestors stormed the fences and rushed onto the field and if looking skywards as a light aircraft buzzed the ground, dropping packets of flour turned you on, then the 1981 tour of New Zealand was the place to be. But for fair-minded people, who were dismayed that rugby football could be the catalyst for such open hostility and violence and the cause of such social disharmony, it is regarded as one of the darkest chapters in the game's history. But it came about because some of rugby's authorities, refused to acknowledge the realities of (then) modern-day life and the forces for social change that were sweeping the world.

The New Zealand RU ignored obvious indications that the tour would lead to trouble. And rugby was lagging miles behind other sports in even considering extending sporting links with the odious apartheid regime back in the Republic.

South Africa had been barred from the Olympics as far back as 1964 and the Basil D'Oliveira affair of 1967 had poisoned cricketing relations. To its shame, New Zealand rugby simply ignored all these things and insisted all was well. That it chose to continue to be associated with the regime in Pretoria through sporting links was a stain on its reputation that would linger for decades.

But when the South Africans arrived in Auckland on 19 July 1981 for their tour, it's safe to say that both they and their hosts were taken aback by the scale and fury of the protests. Their match at Hamilton was called off when 350 protestors swamped the ground just before the start and police took an hour to throw out just fifty of them. Then reports swept the ground that a light aircraft had been hijacked and could be going to crash into the stands. Meanwhile, rugby fans fought with protestors. Later, the scheduled game against South Canterbury at Timaru was cancelled due to police fears that the ground would be impossible to defend.

The next week, there was a sit-down protest in one of the streets in the heart of the capital, Wellington. Peaceful protestors including women were baton-charged by harassed police, while some protestors clearly hijacked the protest to cause their own mischief for other reasons. New Zealand was approaching serious civil disorder.

Somehow, the tour limped on, doing untold damage to New Zealand's worldwide reputation and its own internal harmony.

New Zealand won the first Test, 14-9, in Christchurch but were then hammered 24-12 by the Springboks' revamped team in the second Test at Wellington. Of the provincial teams, only the Maoris could hold the tourists, drawing 12-12 in Napier.

Every other game was won by the South Africans, with the crucial exception of the third and final Test in Auckland. But the match was played out against such absurd scenes and the protests outside the ground were so furious and violent, that rugby came a distant second in terms of interest to all but the blinkered. Flares were hurled across the ground, a light aircraft made dangerously low sorties over the stadium and dropped its flour bombs throughout the game, one of which flattened the All Blacks prop forward Gary Knight.

The two sides reached the end of eighty minutes level at 22-22, the Springbok wing Ray Mordt scoring a hat-trick of tries. But the Welsh referee Clive Norling then played on briefly to cover the time lost when play was halted by the protests. In that short period, South Africa were penalized for a technical infringement and New Zealand full-back Allan Hewson kicked a long-range penalty to win the Test and the series.

But only the blind or the foolish could focus on the rugby. Too much damage had been done to New Zealand's and rugby football's reputations to bother about the games.

You'd have thought that might just have been enough of rugby's links with apartheid South Africa, that the game should have come to its senses. Alas, not so. Shamefully, just as Ireland had done in slipping into the Republic earlier in 1981 for a short tour, England then unbelievably went to South Africa in 1984 for a tour.

Opposite: South Africa's Gerrie Germishuys kicks the ball ahead during a match against Auckland at Eden Park. This controversial tour split New Zealand opinion and cast a shadow over All Black rugby.

The Northern Hemisphere

Back in the northern hemisphere, in the Five Nations Championship, France dominated most of the 1980s. The decade opened with a Grand Slam in each of its first two years. England, at last mustering a proper unit under the inspirational leadership of Bill Beaumont, won in 1980, beating France in Paris and, lastly, Scotland in Edinburgh by 30 points to 18, a match in which the England wing John Carleton scored a hat-trick of tries. Twelve months later, France's formidable forwards beat up everyone to record another Grand Slam.

But the early Eighties also saw a revival in Irish rugby. There hadn't been a great deal for them to cheer about in previous years, with just one title in the previous thirty years of the Championship. But in 1982, Ireland won the Championship and Triple Crown, the following year they shared the title with France and in 1985, they again finished Champions and Triple Crown winners. This was an era of unprecedented success, but one not shared by the 1983 Lions who were led by an Irishman, hooker Ciaran Fitzgerald. They were whitewashed 4-0 in the Test series with the All Blacks, a tour that involved a long, unhappy thirteen week trek.

At the start of the 1984/5 season, Ireland appointed Mick Doyle, a legendary character and man of the game, to be its new coach. There wasn't much subtlety about Doyle's playing philosophy and his teams owed most of their success to the phenomenal goal-kicking of Ollie Campbell. But Doyle's famous mantra of 'Give it a lash, lads' was to become legendary and he received immense plaudits for his bold intentions with a group of players who were, in truth, far from world-beaters.

Another Grand Slam was won in 1984, Scotland's first for fifty-nine years. Peter Dods's phenomenal points scoring was at its heart (he managed 50 in the four matches) and Jim Calder's try in the Grand Slam decider, 'winner takes all' match against France at Murrayfield, was decisive. The previous autumn, England had beaten a weakened New Zealand touring team (Scotland drew with the All Blacks) but the English still won only one of their matches in the New Year's Five Nations.

But a clear trend was emerging. Ollie Campbell was kicking the living daylights out of the ball in Ireland, Dusty Hare was doing likewise for England and the Welsh full-back Gwyn Evans landed six penalty goals for Wales in their 22-12 win over France in 1982. The following year when Ireland beat England 25-15 in Dublin, Campbell and Hare shared ten penalty goals between them. The boot was king and winning ugly was all.

In the great entertainment years of the 1970s, from 1975–9, the dominant sides Wales and France amassed fifty-one tries between them. By grave contrast in the first three years of the next decade, France and Ireland managed a paltry sixteen.

Wales's Paul Thorburn banged over an extraordinary penalty from 71 metres against France at Cardiff in 1986 and the same year, the Hastings brothers, Gavin and Scott, made their debuts for Scotland with Gavin kicking six penalty goals for an 18-17 win over France in Edinburgh. When England beat Wales 21-18 at Twickenham, Rob Andrew landed six penalties and a dropped goal. Tries were becoming endangered species.

Previous pages: England's Bill Beaumont shakes hands with Wales's J. P. R. Williams at the end of the Five Nations match at Cardiff Arms Park in 1981.

The official programme for the 1986 France v All Blacks game. It became known as 'The Battle of Nantes'.

But there was still some fun in the old game. In March 1986, England went to Paris with a side that included a new No. 8 forward, Dean Richards, from the Leicester club. Richards had, in fact, made his debut a fortnight earlier, helping England beat Ireland at Twickenham. When the England party reached Versailles, their traditional base outside the French capital, Richards was paired with one of the old heads in the team, lock forward Maurice Colclough.

They found their room and Colclough flung open the window. Calling Richards to it, he offered him the magnificent vista of Louis the Sun King's fabulous palace laid out in front of them. 'You can get an even better view outside,' advised Colclough. Richards, most inadvisedly, accepted his offer.

No sooner had the burly Richards clambered out than the window slammed shut behind him. Worse still, Colclough raced down the corridor telling his colleagues to keep their windows shut. Richards, meanwhile, found himself perched precariously on a narrow ledge that overlooked a 60-foot plunge to the ground. He was out there a good while before the clowning Colclough relented.

The French hammered England the next day (they would go on to win the Grand Slam the following year) and when the season ended in the northern hemisphere, France headed off on a world tour. It ended in New Zealand where they were beaten

In an era where the boot was king, Ireland owed a lot of their success to the phenomenal goal-kicking of Ollie Campbell.

The programme for the 1987 Australia v New Zealand game at inaugural World Cup.

18-9. But that autumn, five months later, the All Blacks set out on a tour of France. One of the matches was destined to go down in history.

New Zealand beat the French at Toulouse in the first Test and seemed certain to do so again a week later in the second Test. But French coach Jacques Fouroux, who had seen his forwards outplayed in Toulouse, inspired them to such an extent that seven days later they took on the All Blacks in a fearsome physical encounter at Nantes. The match became known forever as 'The Battle of Nantes'.

It isn't every day you pass a medical room, glance in and see a rugby player having his scrotum stitched up. That was the fate of one All Black; most others were battered and smashed to pulp by the pumped up French. France won 16-3 in a match that would prove to be a preview of the following year's World Cup final.

To say the World Cup was planned would be a touch disingenuous. It was forced on the game's hapless administrators, the then largely ineffective IRB, by commercial sharks circling the sport and spying considerable encouragement and enticement from players. For the union's amateur cat was out of the bag and all but gone. When northern hemisphere rugby men arrived in New Zealand in 1987 for the inaugural World Cup, professionalism wasn't so much as obvious as thrust in their faces. New Zealand captain Andy Dalton, who was to miss out on leading his country in the tournament because of injury, was to be seen advertising a tractor on TV. The suits from the IRB wrung their hands in silent fury, knowing full well their impotence at such blatant disregard for the laws of amateurism in the southern hemisphere.

Stories, although of course never proven, of players who were prepared to play on rebel tours of South Africa for financial reward, were equally rife. And Australia was set fair on a similar course. Meanwhile, players in the northern hemisphere like the great Welsh outside-half Jonathan Davies were still being forced to turn professional to earn money, and others were being banned forever for writing books and taking the money. The discrepancy between the hemispheres was stark and alarming.

The first World Cup was a start, not a lot more. New Zealand won it easily, because they only had one serious contest and that was the final against France, which they won 29-9. The All Blacks had blitzed countries like Italy and Fiji by 70 points or more and didn't have any serious opposition even in the quarter-final, where they beat Scotland 30-3, or the semi-final, where they thumped Wales 49-6.

The match of the tournament was a throbbing, pulsating, nerve-tingling semi-final between Australia and France. It contained six tries, huge swings in fortune favouring either side and ended when French full-back Serge Blanco finished off a sweeping move to dive in at the corner with only moments left. The French won 30-24 and Australia's great dream was over. New Zealand won a disappointingly one-sided final 29-9 against a French team that could never scale the similar heights to those it achieved in that stupendous semi-final against Australia. But equally, none could miss the supremacy and style of the New Zealanders. The All Blacks, under the shrewd, calm captaincy of David Kirk, were a smoothly oiled machine of considerable quality.

The World Cup had arrived and rugby had taken an irreversible step towards full professionalism and there would be no turning back.

Previous pages: All Black captain David Kirk goes over for a try during the 1987 Rugby World Cup Final against France. New Zealand won comprehensively 29-9.

Opposite: A battle-scarred David Kirk proudly holds-up the William Webb Ellis trophy.

Andrew Slack
Australia 1978–87
Centre

A Queenslander, he had the distinction of being the first Australian captain to lead the Wallabies to a Grand Slam on a tour of Britain and Ireland in 1984. He made his Test debut in 1978 and played for Australia until the first World Cup in 1987, by which time he had won 39 caps. He was captain nineteen times, from 1984–87. A quiet but shrewd, self-effacing man, he was not a flashy player but a team man and a popular leader.

'The only way you can properly judge an era is by consistency. OK, the Wallabies won in New Zealand in 1949 and did the odd good thing in the 1970s. But we also lost to Tonga in 1973 in Brisbane! However, in the Eighties we were consistent; no one could match that, year in year out. We won not only a large share of our games but also the really important ones. Given that we did that over a period of six to eight years, it's justified in saying things really came together for us for the first time in that period. Of course, we had some special players, which is what you need. You have got to get the right people together. But that was only one factor in the equation. There were some local issues behind it, too. One was the emergence of Queensland as a legitimate counter to New South Wales. Before that, most of the teams in Australian rugby history had been 90 per cent Sydney-based players. But Queensland established a link in the 1970s with Ray Williams, the Welsh coach, and he came out to do coaching and advise us how to go forward. Bob Templeton was responsible for bringing him out and that link began to create something and lift standards.

The other thing Queensland did was establish a relationship with New Zealand. We toured there, and they came to us which meant we were getting good, strong provincial opposition which helped us no end. Suddenly, Queensland began to emerge as a counter to New South Wales and since then there has been a balance in Australian rugby.

Opposite: Australia captain Andy Slack breaks away, watched by England's Bryan Barley.

When you add to those things a pretty good bunch of players who arrived almost together, you see why Australian rugby suddenly emerged as a serious contender on the world stage. There is always talent around but it's about that talent saying, let's keep playing, let's stick together and keep it going longer.

The two main coaches during my time associated with the Wallabies were Bob Dwyer and Alan Jones, both of whom had their strengths. But it's hard to judge completely because you can only do that if you have been in their teams for years. I played a lot for Australia in Jones's time, less so under Dwyer.

Dwyer was what you'd call an "outside the square" thinker. That had its benefits. When I had Dwyer, he was pretty naïve. He came from a club side (Randwick) that had all the superstars and he just thought that transferring all those stars to the international team would work. But of course, it didn't necessarily. The second time he was national coach, at the end of the 1980s, he was much wiser and shrewder.

They were very different personalities. Jones kept his distance from the players whereas Dwyer was much more one of the boys. I always felt Jones was more thorough. His capacity for hard work was like no others and that was contagious.

For me, Jones was the coach that changed the way Australian rugby thought about itself. I don't think there's any doubt of that. Before him, we were always comfortable with playing brilliantly at times. Our backs were great and occasionally, they'd really spark and we'd win well. But Jones was the first person who said, "That's crap. We are going to compete in every area. Not just the backs."

What Jones did in the early 1980s was make us so much more professional in the way we approached everything. There was always a clear analysis of the opposition we were going to play. A tight-head prop knew what sort of a loose-head he was going to face, our scrum-half knew all about his opposite number. Jones would have people looking at everyone. So when we went out for the match every player knew what he was facing. Jones was the one who brought in that professional preparation.

Under him, there wasn't any of the attitude of "Go out and do a bit of training and the rest of the day is yours." Even when you weren't training, Jones wanted you to be resting because he said, "You're international sportsmen: you should consider resting as part of your proper preparation for a match." It took an adjustment on the part of the players to get used to all that and there were difficulties with it. But we weren't stupid, we could see we were getting the results out of it. The methodology was producing the results. So we accepted it and mostly enjoyed it. There was great satisfaction out of winning like that and from working a lot harder than we had in the past.

I'm sure both Alan Jones and Bob Dwyer did many good, important things for Australian rugby. But would they have prospered as they both did without players like Mark Ella, Nick Farr-Jones, 'Campo', Michael Lynagh, Tim Horan and Jason Little?

They both needed quality players to achieve what they did. Yet to be fair, I always thought Jones changed the whole landscape in how the players tended to prepare, so he was the main man here.

I'd agree with the view that not winning the first World Cup was one of the biggest disappointments of my career. It left a hole in my playing record, that's for sure. I was just so disappointed we didn't get to the final, that's the thing that annoys me most about my rugby career. You have to say, we were a team past its best by then and New Zealand were the best side by far. If we had reached that final and played it ten times against the All Blacks, they'd have won eight times. But I'd like to have got there and given it a go.

For me, looking back at those years, the game had an enormous influence on my life. But it's never been my whole life, the complete package. Family means more to me than anything else. It was enjoyable playing rugby and we did have success. I had a great time at school, too. But I remember most the people that I was involved with, not the actual matches and the wins or defeats. They fade in time. But the friendships endure.

A popular team player, Andrew Slack was at the hub of the Australian rugby revolution. Here, he kicks for touch against France.

Danie Gerber
South Africa 1980–92
Centre

Danie Gerber was regarded as one of the greatest centres ever produced by South Africa. Strong, fast and powerful with a devastating hand-off, his career was ruined by the apartheid years in his country.

'I had always wanted to play against the All Blacks, especially in New Zealand. For me, they were the best in the world, the toughest side of all the rugby-playing nations. I had never been to New Zealand and wanted to experience it.

But if I'd known before I left what would happen on that tour, what it was going to be like, maybe I would have stayed at home. One thing's for sure. There will never be a tour like that again. I went just to play rugby, I wasn't interested in the political stuff. I didn't think I'd be afraid of what would happen, I just wanted to play the All Blacks.

But I was afraid, especially when we saw the aeroplane coming low over the ground at Eden Park for the third Test. It was so low that some rugby fans were throwing things at it, although they were warned not to do so. I reckoned I could have hit it if I'd kicked the ball hard enough up into the sky. It didn't seem much higher than the top of the goalposts.

We were worried the plane would get hit or collide with something and crash on the field. By half-time, we were 16-3 down because we'd played the first half facing the direction from which this plane kept coming. And it must have made fifty or sixty sorties low across the ground. When we played with our backs to it in the second half we could focus more on the rugby.

We had an instant introduction into what was going to happen when we first landed in New Zealand at the start of the tour. There were about 3,000–4,000 demonstrators at the airport and they were shouting and screaming. The bus came onto the tarmac to pick us up at the plane, but we could hear them. It was unnerving.

The tour split the New Zealand people in terms of opinion. There were problems throughout the tour and afterwards, too, in the country.

Because of the demonstrations wherever we went, we couldn't use hotels everywhere and some nights we stayed in the local cells at the police station. At least it was safe in there, if not very comfortable on the bunk beds. On other occasions, we'd bed down in the pavilion at some sports ground where they'd installed bunks.

Opposite: On account of apartheid politics Danie Gerber won just 24 caps in twelve years.

Before the first Test in Christchurch, we stayed in a building that housed squash courts. Again, we were camping out on makeshift beds and the mattresses weren't very comfortable. Often the sleeping places were cold and occasionally, we would have to go by bus to the ground at five or six in the morning to avoid demonstrators. That meant a long wait until kick-off at 3 p.m. but we did it. And at some places the New Zealanders put in entertainments for us like pool tables and they cooked us food there. A few of the pavilions became like hotels for us because the police could guarantee security there.

After the match at Hamilton against Waikato was cancelled when the demonstrators broke down fences, invaded the field and threw stones and nails onto the pitch, we were in two minds about whether we would stay or go home. Our management went for a meeting with the police to discuss it. When they got back, they told us there was good news and bad, which did we want first? We said the bad news. It was that the game at Timaru would also have to be cancelled. But the good news was, we were staying and completing the rest of the tour. There was a big roar of relief at that. But it became difficult to concentrate on the rugby. The moment you saw all those demonstrators, you were a bit worried. They were throwing eggs and stuff whenever you went to board your bus. One day, I went out of a hotel to a shop to buy some chocolate. When you went out like that, you could never wear your Springbok blazer, tie or jumper or anything that made it obvious who you were. But a lady and two guys recognized me and three other players I was with (Hennie Becker, Louis Moolman and Divan Serfontein) from photographs I suppose, and they started berating us. They were shouting, "You are racists go home, you have split our country, we don't want you here". It was pretty unpleasant and we had a lot of problems in those circumstances. The people said a lot of terrible things to us and it was quite hard to take.

What these people didn't know, and didn't want to know, was that someone like me had played with black and coloured players in invitation teams for some time. I didn't have a problem playing with them. I also coached rugby and cricket in black townships long before I was a Springbok. But people didn't want to know that. Because of the political situation the New Zealand public who criticized us thought we were against black people all the time. But I couldn't help what my government was doing.

I knew things were wrong in South Africa and that we had to change. But those decisions weren't in my hands or the hands of other Springboks. I'd hoped we would have changed before we did but the politicians did what they wanted.

However, what is also important to remember about that tour is that many New Zealanders were in favour of it. They wanted to help, and they did so by taking us out so we could enjoy ourselves. They are a wonderful people and I have nothing against New Zealanders. We were welcomed by many of them and had some great parties in their company. Perhaps it was ironic but the best party we had on that tour was after the match we'd played against the NZ Maoris. So you couldn't blame 90 per cent of the people. But I understood the views of the protestors. However, I was a rugby player, not a politician.

Could we have won that series? Well, we had our chances in the first Test, but in the final Test I certainly didn't agree with the penalty in injury time that lost us the match and the series. One of their players took a tap penalty and the guy ran at least 15 metres before we tackled him. But the referee gave a penalty and they won the series with it.

I have subsequently come to understand the allegation that it was probably set up that New Zealand had to win the series otherwise there would have been even bigger problems for them. It was important they won that match and the series. The way that last penalty was given suggested that.

Despite his limited Test career, Danie Gerber has, by ratio, the best Springbok try-scoring average, with 19 in 24 Tests.

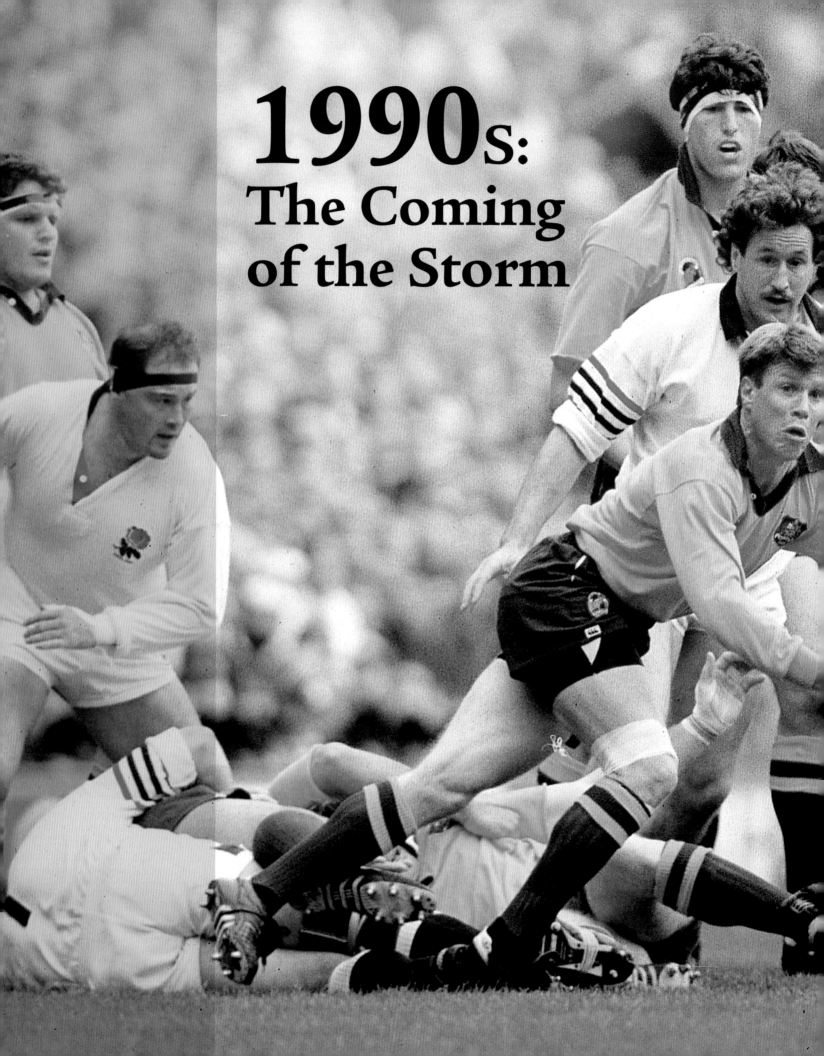

1990s:
The Coming
of the Storm

1990s: The Coming of the Storm

The 1990s was the decade that changed rugby forever. Evolution was replaced by revolution in the game.

The decade began with countries like Ireland making goodwill tours of countries like Namibia (and losing both Tests to them) and ended with most of the rugby-playing world outside the leading nations fearing the effects of professionalism. They had every reason to be concerned.

Paris on a warm August afternoon was the location for rugby union to make history. Given that the French capital had staged Europe's most famous revolution, it somehow seemed an appropriate venue.

In the modest surroundings of the Ambassador hotel in the heart of Paris, a single announcement changed the game forever. It was 26 August 1995, and the then Chairman of the International Rugby Board, Vernon Pugh, made the historic statement in just a single sentence. 'Ladies and Gentlemen, we declare that the game of rugby union is now open.'

> 'Ladies and Gentlemen, we declare that the game of rugby union is now open.'

Just two months earlier, the third Rugby World Cup had been staged in South Africa. It had been a vibrant, colourful, pulsating, controversial success. Things were moving fast in the world and rugby simply reflected that trend.

On the day before the World Cup final in Johannesburg, it was revealed that Rupert Murdoch's News Corporation had offered a sum of around $550 million for television rights to a new Tri-Nations tournament featuring Australia, New Zealand and South Africa. The genie was at last out of the bottle.

Mind you, the cap had been loosened originally, not by a commercial operator like Murdoch but, irony of all ironies, by men who swore they would defend the sport's amateur ethos to their dying day. Officers of the individual unions fiercely upheld the amateur concept on the one hand, yet at the same time invited increasing amounts of sponsors' money into the game. They could not see how one thing would inevitably lead to another.

As the sponsors clambered to get involved with a game of increasing attraction to growing numbers of the general public, the players, those who were the centre of attention, were being told, 'This money has nothing to do with you, it's for the game.'

Such a scenario was naive and absurd: it ignored the ways of the world. Not only did it create resentment in the dressing rooms of the senior game, but the increased demands from countries that their players spend ever more time preparing and playing the game to elevate standards still further, caused deeper dismay. The consequences of this state of affairs was blindingly obvious to everyone, it seemed, except those who ran the home unions in the northern

New Zealand wing John
Kirwan attempts to break
through the Australian defence
during the 1991 World
Cup semi-final match at
Lansdowne Road, Dublin.

hemisphere, in countries like England, Scotland and Ireland. The Welsh had
always been a tad more realistic and as for the French, well, the joke was, they
just carried on paying their players.

In the southern hemisphere, far away from the IRB's home base, it was another
story. Here, realism had dawned many years earlier. It was considered simply a
matter of time before the whole amateur edifice collapsed. It was already cracking
and crumbling. What was certain to bring it down was the advent of a World
Cup, which had started back in 1987. Perhaps only a sport as conservative as
rugby union could have stumbled and staggered through another eight years of
denial before reality was finally grasped.

There was, in effect, a sham through the first half of the 1990s. Gala dinners
to raise money for players' funds were being organized in southern hemisphere
countries, where generous expenses being paid were already the equivalent of a
wage. Rugby union had become professional in all but name.

The second World Cup in 1991 was hosted by the Five Nations Championship
countries. This meant games were played all over Britain, Ireland and France
in such widespread locations as Bayonne, Béziers, Belfast, Pontypridd,
Llanelli, Leicester, Lille, Lansdowne Road, Edinburgh, Gloucester, Cardiff and
Twickenham. This was casting the net too far.

But it was a tournament lit up by the dazzling back play of Australia, the
eventual winners, most notably in their semi-final victory over New Zealand in

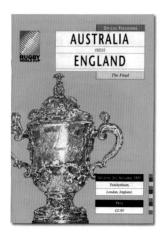

The official programme for the 1991 Rugby World Cup final Australia v England.

Dublin. The genius of David Campese was at its zenith that day; his arcing run from the unfamiliar fly-half position taking him outside the New Zealand defence for a memorable try, and his scintillating break down the right and mesmerizing flipped pass putting Tim Horan over for another. New Zealand couldn't live with that kind of brilliance.

Indeed, David Campese was dragging the old game, almost single-handedly at times it seemed, out of its amateur ethos towards the new dawn of entertainment, personality and mass media coverage. After all, 'Campo' had been visiting Italy in the northern hemisphere winters since the mid-1980s to play club rugby. It's safe to say he wasn't there just to endure the freezing Milanese winters.

Campese epitomized rugby's march towards the alluring lights of its professional future. This complex character from Australia – derided as a loud-mouth by those who didn't know him, but respected as often shy and self-effacing by those who really did, was undoubtedly the chief playing figure of his era. For entertainment, buzz and excitement, no one could match him when he got the ball. Invariably, something extraordinary would happen.

Of course, Campese made mistakes. But then, most geniuses are flawed in some respects. Study the bigger picture, the wider scenario and you see the enormous benefits. As ever, Australia's 1991 World Cup winning coach Bob Dwyer hit the nail on the head when asked once how he coached a maverick talent such as Campese.

'Mate, I make it a policy of mine never to interfere with bloody genius.'

Dwyer, now back in charge of the Wallabies, retorted, 'Mate, I make it a policy of mine never to interfere with bloody genius.' How right he was, especially considering the fact that Campese himself often admitted that he never quite knew which way his mind and legs would take him on a rugby field. If he wasn't certain, how could any coach make complex plans for him? Dwyer's genius was that he allowed Campese's brilliance to flow largely uninhibited. Australia won the World Cup due in large part to that fact.

England, by complete contrast, had ground their way to the final by means of a hard, physical, forward-orientated 19-10 win over France in Paris and a dour 9-6 kick-riddled game against Scotland in Edinburgh. The Paris spectacle was enlivened by the sight of the brilliant French full-back Serge Blanco punching an opponent and, later, the French coach Daniel Dubroca allegedly assaulting, the referee.

The final was played at Twickenham in front of Her Majesty The Queen. Maybe it was the presence of royalty, maybe Campese's goading remarks in the week leading up to the match. But whatever the cause, England bizarrely abandoned their focus on hard-driving forward play, which had taken them to the final (and Grand Slam in the 1991 Five Nations Championship), and attempted a glitzy, ambitious game plan based around backs who were not used to such a glut of possession in their hands. Not surprisingly, they ran the wrong lines, drifted across field incessantly, failed to break the gain line or penetrate properly, and fumbled frequently.

All this simply played into Australia's hands for the Wallabies forwards were in no way the equal of the England pack. Had England driven the ball up strongly off the

Opposite: John Eales and Tony Daley celebrate Australia's victory over England at Twickenham in the 1991 World Cup Final. The despondent England captain Will Carling can be seen in the background.

fringes, dominated first phase and kicked for position, they would almost certainly have overpowered and strangled the life out of the Australians. A World Cup final must first be won, then analysed for style marks, not the other way round.

As it was, England threw away a World Cup that was theirs for the taking. But they reaffirmed their power and quality by winning a second successive Grand Slam in the 1992 Five Nations Championship three months later.

One momentous event seemed to follow another in this decade. On 11 February 1990, Nelson Mandela had walked out of jail in South Africa a free man, to the delight of the democratic world. The collapse of the old guard in South African politics heralded a new era for the country, and also for the Springboks.

A Stranger Returns

In most countries, the long years of isolation would have meant a painful process of gradual and frustrating rebuilding. Therefore, when the Springboks reappeared on the world stage, they were horribly exposed. In 1992, they lost 33-16 to England at Twickenham and then 26-3 to the new world champions Australia in Cape Town. The critics and pessimists on the high veld forecast years of such humiliations. Yet the same year, when New Zealand went to Johannesburg, they only just sneaked home 27-24. The green shoots of a Springbok recovery could already be detected, and they were confirmed when South Africa beat France in Lyon 20-15 at the end of that first year back. France won the second Test in Paris, 29-6, to square the series but it was obvious that the pace of the South African rugby recovery was gathering momentum.

In 1994, the Springboks hosted England, losing the first Test in Pretoria 32-15, but winning in Cape Town, 27-9. It was a tour sullied by violence in the match against Eastern Province at Port Elizabeth, when Tim Rodber was sent off and Jonathan Callard had his face and eye kicked by a local player, causing twenty-five stitches to be inserted. Unhappily, the culprit got away with it.

Later that year, the Springboks returned to the northern hemisphere for a proper tour, beating Wales 20-12 and Scotland 34-10. But it wasn't just the results that mattered.

World rugby had been denuded by the Springboks' isolation. The banishment was deserved but the game in general suffered, there was no doubt of that. At a glittering reception at an elegant Scottish country house outside Edinburgh in the week leading up to the Springboks first international against Scotland for twenty-five years, kilts and tartan jackets mixed freely once again with those wearing Springbok blazers. Beside crackling log fires, it felt fantastic to all who were there the night that South African rugby had come in from the cold.

Steadily, inexorably through these early matches, South Africa was finding the core of a team for the 1995 World Cup. True, they flopped in New Zealand in 1994, in a poor series. But the nucleus was being assembled, and none could dispute the talent available. Led by François Pienaar in the back row, there were forwards of proper substance like the Natal lock Mark Andrews and renowned scrummager

Balie Swart in the front row, Chester Williams and James Small on the wings, Japie Mulder at centre and the man dubbed 'The Rolls-Royce of full-backs' André Joubert. Others, like the brilliantly talented scrum-half Joost van der Westhuizen and flanker Ruben Kruger, would be added soon.

The 2-0 Test series defeat in New Zealand with the last Test drawn cost coach Ian McIntosh and manager Jannie Engelbrecht, two of South African rugby's most revered figures, their jobs, both being dismissed by the volatile South African Rugby president, Louis Luyt. In came Kitch Christie and Morne du Plessis as coach and manager respectively. The scene was set for a South-African hosted World Cup in 1995.

To this day, it remains one of the best, surpassed only by the Australian-hosted event of 2003. The sun shone, the light was exceptional, the nation was captivated and visitors were welcomed regally (excepting the poor unfortunates who were

Scotland captain Gavin Hastings tries to power through South Africa's Ruben Kruger and Pieter Hendriks during the Springboks tour of Great Britain and Ireland in 1994.

victims of violence, mainly in Johannesburg). None who were in the Republic between the day of the first match, 25 May, through to the final on 24 June, could fail to grasp the bosom-like relationship between white South Africans and rugby football. Everywhere you went, most people you talked to had just one topic of conversation on their lips: the Rugby World Cup.

Australia, the defending champions, still had their 1991 winning coach Bob Dwyer in charge and they also retained several star players like Campese, Lynagh, Little, Horan, Eales, Kearns, Ofahengaue and McKenzie. They had added the likes of George Gregan and Matthew Burke, players who would in time become star names themselves. But the Wallabies didn't quite have it up front. They lost their opening match to South Africa, a tension filled affair at Newlands Stadium, Cape Town, by 27 points to 18 and then were felled by England in the quarter-finals, but only 25-22 because of a last minute drop goal from 45 metres by England fly-half Rob Andrew.

But one man seized the 1995 World Cup by the scruff of its neck. He wasn't English or Australian, nor even a South African. He was a New Zealander, he was just 20 years old and his name was Jonah Lomu. A physical colossus, an absolute

Rob Andrew lands the vital drop goal in the 1995 Rugby World Cup quarter-final against Australia to win the game 25-22.

freak at 6 ft 5 ins tall and 18 stone 8 lb in weight, Lomu went through the world's leading rugby nations at that World Cup like a combine harvester through a field of corn. Anything standing was razed to the ground.

He scored two tries in the All Blacks' 43-19 demolition of Ireland and if he wasn't scoring tries himself, he was making them for others. Mercifully, he didn't play when New Zealand beat Japan 145-17 in their group match. If he had, it would probably have been closer to 200.

Results such as that, and Scotland's 89-0 flogging of the Ivory Coast, revealed how weak some of rugby's lower tiers really were. The tragic accident suffered by the Ivory Coast wing Max Brito in the 1995 tournament underlined the dangers of such mis-matches.

Brito was playing for his country in their final pool match against Tonga at Rustenburg. He went to pick up a loose ball, slipped and was engulfed by the big, physical Tongan players arriving for the ball. When the ball was released, Brito was seen laying motionless on the ground. He never moved again. The young man had suffered a horrifying paralysis rendering him a quadriplegic for the rest of his life.

Brito was flown to hospital, comforted as far as possible and eventually flown back to France. One month after the World Cup had ended, I walked into his hospital room at a clinic in the suburbs of Bordeaux. There he lay, from outward appearances his lean body a testimony to his sporting fitness. But alas, he could move barely a finger, certainly not an arm. He was helpless; fed by his carers, cleaned by them and with the prospect of spending the remainder of his life in such a state.

> 'I am a man at peace with myself, I am not stressed ... I do not blame rugby for this, it can happen to anyone for the neck is so fragile.'

We talked briefly, through an interpreter, and his words were whispered, halting. The emotion of the occasion was haunting. I resolved to return at a later date. When I did, a year or more later, he had retrieved just the slightest movement in one hand, but in reality desperately little. But he had by then formulated his thoughts.

'There have been very, very depressing moments, truly black times particularly at the beginning. I believe everybody in this situation must go through that phase.

'You cross periods that are mentally very delicate and which lead you to think of suicide. It is a watershed, a necessary stage that one gets over or doesn't. It is a traumatic event in your life but you have to come to terms with it and that takes time.'

The experience gave Max Brito a perspective on life few ever encompass. 'I see people getting angry for such small, insignificant reasons. So many problems between people could be avoided. Most are really not very important anyway. When I see children dying and starving on TV and then hear people arguing about petty things, it makes me laugh bitterly. There are many hard things in life, things that need more attention.'

And his own situation? 'I am a man at peace with myself, I am not stressed,' he said. 'I do not blame rugby for this, it can happen to anyone for the neck is so fragile.'

The calm dignity and the logical reasoning he offered somehow intensified the awful sadness.

Scotland caught the full force of the typhoon known as Jonah Lomu in their 1995 World Cup quarter-final against the All Blacks. Lomu scored only one try but his powerful running and coruscating hand-offs caused chaos in the Scottish defence. It finished 48-30, respectable enough on the scoreboard, but New Zealand's 45-16 lead at one stage was a better indication of their superiority. That, allied to England's dramatic late win over Australia, paired the two nations in the semi-final. The pre-match hype and build-up was not a wasted exercise – this proved to be one of the defining games of any World Cup.

In the very first minute, Lomu picked up the ball for the first time, smashed through the attempted tackle of Tony Underwood, gathered sufficient speed to outpace the covering England captain Will Carling and then simply ran straight through and over full-back Mike Catt to score a stunning, staggering try of pace and enormous power. That single act defined the game and also decided it. England had the look of rabbits caught in a car's headlights writ large upon their faces. Even at that early stage, you knew there was no way back for them.

New Zealand finished with 45 points, Lomu with four tries and England (who somehow scored 29) with bruises all over their bodies. But the great man himself would come to regret not the tries but the fuss and adulation it created throughout the rugby-playing world. He said after the tournament, 'It is horrible to be this well known. Fame is highly overrated. I could do without it all really; it makes me feel very uncomfortable.' It was

In a demonstration of his immense power and pace All Black Jonah Lomu evades a challenge from Rob Andrew during the 1995 Rugby World Cup semi-final. New Zealand cruised to victory 45-29.

something Lomu was going to have to learn to live with throughout his entire career.

In the other semi-final, meanwhile, South Africa had survived a Durban deluge as well as everything the French could hurl at them, to win a match played in appalling conditions.

In the event, the French went within literally an inch of spoiling South Africa's party. That was how close one of their forwards came to a touchdown that would have ended the Springboks' hopes. In the event, South Africa squelched home 19-15 and the 50,000 crowd then attempted to do likewise.

Durban airport became the focus of the entire country. Planes were lined up like buses outside a football ground. In the end, the ground staff simply couldn't cope. Allocated seats became a fantasy and when the doors of the terminal were opened leading to the planes, a rush ensued. Those first on seized the first class seats and swilled champagne all the way down to Cape Town. Flights were still arriving there at nearly two o'clock in the morning. But somehow, South Africa coped.

How the Springboks would cope in the final with Lomu and the dominant New Zealanders who had played by far the best rugby of the tournament, was

Joost van der Westhuizen feeds his backs during South Africa's semi-final clash with France.

Following pages: Two great rugby superpowers line-up prior to 1995 World Cup final.

another matter. There were fewer true stars in the South African fifteen but what they did have was a real team.

Nelson Mandela had spoken of the Rainbow Nation and its representatives in the famous green jerseys now offered up their lives for victory in the final.

Bodies were hammered at every turn, limbs bashed and skin cut. Still the South Africans would not take a backward step. Lomu invariably received the ball with two or three Springboks attached to it. Even if he made a little progress, he would be brought down by another kamikaze tackle from an opponent. South Africa tackled until they dropped and then they tackled on their knees.

In the end, six kicks produced a 9-9 stalemate at the end of normal time and extra time was played. Not a try in sight but the drama was gripping. Andrew Mehrtens edged the All Blacks ahead again at 12-9, Joel Stransky replied to tie it all up at 12-12 and it was still anyone's Cup and glory. And then came the denouement. Stransky, as calm and unflustered as a businessman at his desk on a normal day, dropped a soaring goal to put South Africa ahead 15-12.

It was the signal for a furious and frantic assault by New Zealand in the final eight minutes. They tried everything, but were repelled by some of the most courageous, heart-stopping tackling and defensive covering the great game had ever seen. The final whistle from English referee Ed Morrison triggered jubilation throughout the new South Africa, whose celebrations were led by Mandela, wearing a replica No. 6 Springbok jersey, on the pitch at Ellis Park. It became the symbolic emblem of the whole World Cup.

Afterwards, there would be bitter accusations by the New Zealanders that their food had been tampered with. That explained, they said, why most of their team had been sick the night before the final. Whatever the truth, most of the world smiled almost as brightly as the South

The official programme for the 1995 Rugby World Cup final between New Zealand and South Africa.

Africans at the image of Mandela and his country's triumph. It didn't need any words to remind the world that because of isolation this was the first World Cup South Africa had competed in, and they'd won the glittering trophy at the first attempt.

But alas, subtlety and Louis Luyt remained as far apart as heaven and hell. At the after-match banquet, the South African Rugby president stood up and lived down to everyone's expectations by boasting that the Springboks would have won the 1987 and 1991 tournaments, too, had they been allowed to participate. It was an ungracious, arrogant piece of invective that soured the occasion but not the victory for a reborn South Africa.

But then, world rugby had been warned about Louis Luyt well before the first ball was kicked at the 1995 World Cup. The South African said in one interview prior to the tournament: 'The 1991 World Cup in England was laughable. There seems to be a great problem with the Five Unions who can't seem to agree on anything. They were fighting over who was allowed to wear World Cup blazers and they'd spend bloody hours discussing petty matters such as who qualified to go to dinners and who could sit nearest the Queen. It was all very petty.'

Demonstrating the impact rugby can have, Nelson Mandela congratulates François Pienaar on winning the World Cup, beckoning a new era for a united South Africa.

Professionalism Arrives

It seemed impossible for the game to trump that wonderful World Cup for major news. But the IRB managed it with aplomb less than two months later when they dropped the bombshell that the old game was no more. Professionalism was now permitted.

The great irony of the situation was that very few people had a clue exactly what it would mean, or how to proceed. But a few smart operators did. English agent Mike Burton, known for years as the 'King of the Tickets', answered a telephone in his West Country office the very next morning following the announcement. It was from a Scottish international player who said simply, 'Burto, you'd better represent me. I haven't got a clue what to ask my club for, so can you handle it.'

Even Burton confessed later he didn't have much idea either about the going rate for a club player. After all, in his business, market prices dictated. But what Burton was switched on to was the fact that a great deal would be different within twelve months. So those players whom he signed up were strongly advised to sign only an initial 1-year contract. That, he smiled, provided everyone with the chance to negotiate another deal just twelve months later.

It was a brilliant piece of advice. The Rugby Football Union had greeted the news from Paris with a decision typical of their long experience of inertia. They declared a 12-month moratorium in which the respective parties could wait, assess, analyse and decide the best way forward. Unfortunately, this ensured chaos would reign within the English game for the next twelve years.

However, it has now emerged, the much maligned gentlemen at Twickenham may have been rather more savvy than they received credit for at the time. It is alleged they instructed Don Rutherford, their Director of Rugby, to go out and sign up the leading English players. That, it was felt, would at least guarantee some semblance of order in the months and years ahead that most people could see would be fraught with difficulties.

But Rutherford was of the old school. He'd been a British and Irish Lion as far back as 1966 in New Zealand and played all his career in an amateur sport. He had graduated to a top position at Twickenham without departing for experience in the world outside rugby, the business environment. Thus, Rutherford, subsequent allegations have claimed, did nothing. The top English players were not signed up.

The field was left at the mercy of shrewd, tough businessmen like Sir John Hall, the owner of Newcastle United Football Club. Hall extended his sporting domain to take in Newcastle rugby club and he immediately raided the successful Wasps club in North London to offer their fly-half Rob Andrew a five-year contract worth a reported £750,000. These were fantasy figures in a sport that had still been supposedly amateur less than a year earlier. Andrew took the first available means of transport north and signed on the dotted line, soon to be followed by his Wasps team-mates Dean Ryan and Steve Bates. The great player chase had begun.

Hulking great second row forwards and tight-head props with cauliflower ears, who had spent their whole playing lives getting bashed black and blue and then being asked to pay their club's subs for the privilege, suddenly found themselves in great demand. The old order had been swept away: money was pouring into the game.

Not very special players were, quite soon, to be seen driving around their towns in very special cars indeed. Rugby's metamorphosis from quaintly amateur and idealistic to the latest proponent of 20th-century commercialism had happened with brutal speed. Calamitous, as it was to turn out.

Dick Best saw both sides of the coin. A man of rugby all his life, Best had played most of his career with the London club Harlequins and then taken up coaching, a well-trodden path. Of course, in those early days of a coach's life, he was rushing out of work as quickly as possible to try and avoid the worst of the evening rush hour, getting down to his club, donning training gear and helping shoo the players out of the warm dressing rooms into an invariably eerily lit ground where the cold gripped everyone daft enough to be out there.

Best says, 'When I look back, it was incredible the amount of time we were giving up to the game. In 1988, for example, I was coaching Harlequins, Middlesex, London, Division, England Under 21s and, the following year, England "A". I spent my whole life coaching and holding down a day job as well. Now, I can't believe I did it and I shouldn't think anyone else all around the world can believe what they did, either. It was almost surreal what you gave up to do it.'

> 'I spent my whole life coaching and holding down a day job as well. Now, I can't believe I did it and I shouldn't think anyone else all around the world can believe what they did either.'

Under Best, his teams enjoyed much success. Harlequins won the English Cup and the divisional championship. He also coached the London Division side that beat the touring Australians at Twickenham, in 1988. Under Best, London played a brand of rugby that involved attacking opponents, not looking for the safety-first method. Thus, when Roger Uttley bowed out of his coaching role with England at the end of 1991, Best was a logical choice to replace him.

He took the job on the understanding that he would be allowed to formulate an attacking strategy for the team and have sole charge of selection. England had been inconsistent performers for years and only rarely produced a type of rugby worth getting excited about. True, they had won the coveted Grand Slam in 1991, but only through a turgid combination of massive forward power and goal kicking. But the arrival the following year of Best, never a man afraid to speak his mind, ensured things would change.

In 1992, England won a second successive Grand Slam, the first time they had done that for sixty-eight years. This time, they played a compelling brand of free-flowing rugby with a high rhythm and pace. No one in the northern hemisphere could handle that; indeed, they beat France eight times in succession between 1989 and 1995, an extraordinary sequence of results. Nor could the South Africans handle it when they went to Twickenham in 1992, finishing heavy losers by 33 points to 16. Not even the All Blacks could hold England, going down 15-9 at Twickenham in 1993. It was a golden era, that was for sure.

Best remembers: 'That victory over the All Blacks created an extraordinary out-pouring of emotion. We drove to a dinner at the London Guildhall after the game and people were dancing half-naked in the streets, waving England flags and scarves. There were unbelievable scenes. I thought then that we had really uncorked something special.'

Yet England's great team was soon to be in decline, with several key players like Wade Dooley and Peter Winterbottom about to retire.

England had gone to Dublin in early 1993 as hot favourites to beat Ireland. Bookmakers were famously offering 10-1 on England to win. The result was an unforgettable: Ireland 17 England 3. 'And lucky to get the three' said Best, ruefully. In Ireland that night, the celebrations began at once and were still going on sometime later.

England also lost to Wales in that Championship, 10-9 at Cardiff, after a defensive aberration by Rory Underwood was seized upon by Wales's inspirational wing Ieuan Evans. Suddenly, England had lost two games and the knives were out for their coach.

One of England's most inventive, attacking minded coaches, Dick Best was extraordinarily fired by England despite winning 14 of the 17 matches during his tenure.

'There was an outcry, people were saying "Why are we losing games"? People were being rude to my wife of the time in the supermarket, it was extraordinary,' remembered Best. 'One guy went up to her and told her I was a w*****. She said "You tell him that yourself. But he'll punch your lights out".'

Best had been asked to go on the British and Irish Lions tour of New Zealand that summer as assistant coach to Ian McGeechan. So he flew home from Dublin with England on the Sunday morning and went straight into a selection meeting at Heathrow airport to choose the Lions squad.

In the event, the Lions lost the series 2-1 that year, but only after what they regarded as a dreadful piece of refereeing that cost them victory 20-18 in the first Test at Christchurch. They won the second Test comfortably but lost the third, heavily.

'We got cheated out of the first Test by the referee giving a penalty to New Zealand right at the end,' Best alleged. 'We blew them away in the second Test but they bounced back well in the last one. It was very disappointing; that should have been only the second Lions team that century to win a series in New Zealand.'

Best had been working for a travel company in Twickenham and his name as England coach was an undoubted attraction to them. His coaching tenure, from late 1991 to mid-1994, spanned seventeen matches of which England won fourteen, a supreme effort. Yet with the 1995 World Cup less than a year away, Best went home one evening to be told that Graham Smith, the chairman of the RFU's coaching sub-committee, was waiting for him in his living room. That wasn't a complete surprise because Smith's wife was godmother to one of Best's children. But when England's coach walked into the room, he knew instantly why Smith was there. One look at his face told me, before he'd said a word. He just said the committee felt it was time for a change. 'When I look back now and think that firing was brought about because we lost two matches, I am left scratching my head.' The early 1990s had been crucial years for England. Best explained 'Geoff Cooke was instrumental in laying the groundwork for so much of what England went on to achieve. He brought a background of sports science to the game, which people had never understood and we got much better organized, although it was still technically in the amateur era.'

Within almost weeks of losing the England job, Best's old club Harlequins had stepped in to sign him up. Seeing the way the game was going, they made him English rugby's first fully paid Director of Rugby. The new era had begun.

'I thought, why not? I'd been working all hours trying to do a day job and then coaching all over the place, followed by travelling at weekends. It was a hell of a commitment. The 'Quins offer meant that I'd be paid well for doing a job I had been doing for years for nothing. It was a no-brainer, really.'

Best saw close-up the way the RFU floundered when professionalism was announced, like a bolt from the blue. 'They'd all been cocooned inside their own little private worlds; they didn't understand that this was now a potentially huge commercial sport with important business decisions to be taken. They could have signed up the best 120 players to the Union and they'd have had control ever after.

> ## 'You tell him yourself. But he'll punch your lights out.'

Previous pages: Ireland's hero Eric Elwood is held aloft after their historic victory over England (17–3) in the 1993 Five Nations. The victory prompted jubilant celebrations.

Opposite: British and Irish Lion's lock Wade Dooley wins a line-out in the 1993 tour of New Zealand.

But by the time their twelve months moratorium had ended, the horse had bolted.

'It meant that English rugby spent the next decade involved in a fight for its leading players. The RFU had their chance but Sir John Hall was the first man in and he set a template for others to follow.'

Best insists that professionalism should have been introduced in a milder form far earlier than 1995. 'It ought to have been done in stages, first at international level then down the levels to club rugby, to give countries a chance to adapt and sort out the problems as they went along.' Instead, it came overnight.

Even a man with extensive business experience in a variety of fields like Dick Best found it bewildering. 'I was suddenly given a budget of £2.5 million by 'Quins and told to go and get on with it. I found it almost frightening.'

Almost at once, Best flew to Ireland to talk with a player whom he'd heard good things about. 'I sat down with him and talked terms. I offered him £35,000 a year and he bit both my arms off. He got that because he was an Irish international: England internationals were on £50,000!

'I went back to Harlequins, announced it to the board and said I had certificates from his surgeon proving his knees were OK, despite the injuries he'd had. I told them "You're going to have to bear with me on this one. I have a feeling about this guy, I think he could be a world beater."

'The board said it all looked very dodgy and they didn't like the sound of it at all. But he didn't turn out to be too bad a player. I always rated Keith Wood.'

Clubs in England were starting to throw money at almost anything that moved. Best said, 'It was like Disneyland; business money was being chucked around everywhere. People in rugby didn't understand what professionalism meant. No one understood, it was a process of adaptation. And that included the players. They thought being professional meant just picking up a vast salary each month and swanning around the place. They didn't understand that professional sportsmen rested in their spare time, prepared their minds and bodies for matches. It was an alien world and they needed educating fast.'

But if the emergence of professionalism was causing chaos in some countries of the world, in the southern hemisphere the transition was a lot smoother. In reality, countries like New Zealand, South Africa and Australia had dipped their toes in the professional water in some form or another for several years. The players in the British Isles and Ireland had looked upon this with a mixture of envy and frustration. A more liberal attitude and a grasp of greater reality had been apparent in the southern hemisphere. Rupert Murdoch's multimillion dollar contract offer for Tri-Nations rugby did not begin this progress, it exacerbated it. And the constant on-off rumours of a professional rugby circus being set up by the likes of Kerry Packer had accustomed those who administered the game in the southern hemisphere to the reality that full-blown professionalism was simply a matter of time, an inevitability.

Undoubtedly, the sanctioning of a World Cup in the sport had ensured the floodgates would eventually open to the complete commercialism of the game. Once that had happened, there could be no turning back. But there was another great benefit to the game throughout the world arising from that tournament.

Forgotten Friends and a Changing Game

The so-called 'second tier' rugby nations, the likes of Japan, Canada, Samoa, Fiji, Argentina, the USA, Romania and Italy, suddenly thought they spied a route onto the game's world stage. Some were right. The Italians had been playing rugby in a tiny oasis amid a soccer-mad country for many years. But after the arrival of the Rugby World Cup, it was only another thirteen years before they were invited to participate in the International Championship, which was promptly expanded to six nations.

This was a thoroughly healthy, exciting by-product of the opening up of a game that had been closed off, like a secret club, for too many years. Wales had been among the first of the senior rugby-playing nations to discover that these so-called 'second tier' rugby nations could pack a powerful punch, figuratively speaking. In the 1991 Rugby World Cup, the Welsh played Western Samoa at Cardiff and promptly lost, 16-13.

'Lucky we weren't playing the whole of Samoa,' said one wag. But it proved that countries like Samoa, Argentina and Italy had much to offer the wider rugby-playing world. Until the Rugby World Cup, all they had lacked was a stage on which to demonstrate the point.

Romania was another nation that had upset several of the traditional rugby-

In a statement of intent, Western Samoa triumph over Wales at Cardiff 16-13 in the 1991 World Cup. 'Lucky we weren't playing the whole of Samoa,' joked one Welsh fan.

playing nations. They beat Wales in 1983 and 1988, Scotland in 1984 and 1991. Then in 1998, Scotland fell to Italy in Treviso and the same year, suffered a 51-26 hiding at the hands of the Fijians in Suva.

As for Argentina, they beat England in Buenos Aires in 1990 and repeated the feat seven years later, this time by a whopping 33 points to 13. In 1994, the Pumas beat Scotland 2-0 in a Test series in Buenos Aires and then won at Murrayfield in 1999.

Ireland, too, suffered their setbacks at the hands of these newer rugby nations. Namibia beat them twice in 1991 on their tour of southern Africa, they went down 40-25 to Samoa in Dublin in 1996, and lost three matches on the trot to Italy, 22-12 in 1995 and then 37-29 and 37-22 in 1997.

As for France, they even managed to lose to Tonga on their South Pacific tour in 1999. They also lost to Argentina in 1992 and Canada in 1994.

Another significant benefit of rugby union's move to professionalism was that no longer would so many of the best union players defect to rugby league. By the end of 1994, rugby union had seen very significant numbers of its finest players cross over to the professional code. Players like the great Welshmen Lewis Jones and David Watkins had gone years earlier, followed by others like England prop Mike

Speed in motion. New Zealand's Jonah Lomu sets off for the line, chased by French wing Philippe Bernat-Salles, one of the fastest players of his generation. France won the game 43-31.

Coulman, Ireland's brilliant No. 8 Ken Goodall and other Welsh players like John Bevan and Keith Jarrett. England had lost the formidably fast wing Martin Offiah who became one of the top rugby league players in the world.

But it was Australia who traditionally lost most of their best union players. They suffered not so much the loss of a dribble of talent but a flood tide. Indeed, the union game was constantly weakened in that country by seeing its best players change codes. Rugby league became all embracing, much the more powerful of the two games. As fast as rugby union unearthed a superb talent, players like Ken Wright, Ricky Stuart, Ray Price, Michael O'Connor and countless others, they were snapped up by rugby league. Professionalism, when it came in rugby union in 1995, made a huge difference to Australian rugby. Indeed, up to the start of 2007, Australia were still the only country to have won two World Cups.

The steady flow of players worldwide to rugby league continued right up into the early 1990s. Indeed, as late as December 1994, *Rugby World* magazine put pictures of fourteen leading players on its cover, all of whom had gone to league. They were as follows: John Devereux, Scott Quinnell, Richard Webster, Scott Gibbs and Jonathan Davies (all Wales), John Gallagher, Frano Botica, Craig Innes, Va'aiga Tuigamala (all New Zealand), Alan Tait (Scotland), Jim Fallon and Martin Offiah (England) and the Australians Ricky Stuart and Garrick Morgan. But this was only a small selection from the numbers making the switch and the magazine asked 'How much longer can rugby union go on losing these players?'

But the move to professionalism in 1995 changed everything. The loss of talent virtually ceased overnight. And over the years, the growing profile of the now professional Wallabies even allowed rugby union to make inroads into league's ascendancy in Australia. Rugby union was seen as by far the more competitive international sport and the trend began to be reversed. Now rugby league is losing some of its star men, like Lote Tuqiri, Henry Paul, Scott Gibbs, Andy Farrell and Chev Walker.

In its new guise as a professional sport, rugby union the world over quickly began to understand one thing. Pre-planning was essential, on and off the field. No country could any longer be run along the quaint old haphazard lines of its amateur past. Proper structures and paid employees had to be put in place to ensure the game went into this harsh new commercial world organized and able to adapt.

But too many of the officials continuing to try and run the unions were blunderers. England, for example, decided in 1996 that selling off the rights to televize their home games in the Five Nations Championship to satellite television, would be a brilliant wheeze. Traditionally, all matches in the tournament had been on the BBC, terrestrial television, with the widest possible audience.

Twickenham weren't interested in continuing to ensure everyone could see matches; all they wanted was more money. This philosophy has been at the heart of the English RFU ever since. The fact that England didn't actually own the rights for their home games concerned no one at Twickenham. But when the Celtic countries rose in fury and slung them out of the Championship, they did become rather more concerned.

The official programme for the 1998 France v England game.

Following pages: Australia celebrate Owen Finegan's try against France during the 1999 World Cup Final at the Millennium Stadium in Cardiff.

Opposite: Australian lock John Eales, one of the game's great representatives, powers through a French challenge in the 1999 World Cup final. Australia won the game 35-12.

Eventually, after long months of accusations and counter-claims, RFU officials had to go cap in hand to their Celtic rivals and plead for reinstatement. So the 1997 Five Nations went ahead, but so much bad feeling had been created by the affair that no one spied the arrival of a golden French era. France won the 1997 and 1998 Five Nations Championships with a Grand Slam each year. And how they merited them.

In 1997, France went to Ireland and won 32-15, followed by a 23-20 win at Twickenham and a 27-22 win over Wales in Paris. The coveted Slam was completed in glorious style, a 47-20 thrashing of Scotland in the fiftieth and final Five Nations game to be played at the atmospheric Parc des Princes.

In 1998, France started with a 24-17 win over England in Paris and then went to Murrayfield, so often a graveyard for French hopes, and won 51-16. Two weeks later, with glorious French unpredictability, they confronted Ireland in Paris as 33-1 on favourites and only just stumbled home 18-16. Ireland led until seven minutes from the end. Suitably chastised, the French went to Wembley where Wales were playing their home games due to work on the new Millennium Stadium.

There was no lack of support for the Welsh in their temporary home; there just weren't any Welsh points to cheer that day. Alas, there were a few by France: 51 in all. Seven golden tries lit up a match that was a throwback to years of brilliant flowing rugby hallmarked by the French. Ironically, one of the few players who didn't score that day was one of those chiefly responsible for France's back-to-back Grand Slams, the exciting, flying wing Philippe Bernat-Salles, who was known as the 'Pau Rocket'. The inventive Thomas Castaignède set alight the blue touchpaper that day and the explosion was wondrous to behold. Even the Welsh admired it, painful as it was to see.

In 1997, the British and Irish Lions, coached again by that shrewd Scot Ian McGeechan and managed by the equally wily Fran Cotton, went to South Africa and won the three-match Test series 2-1. South African rugby had declined since its famous World Cup win: in 1996, New Zealand had won a Test series in South Africa (2-1) for the first time in their history. Given that they had been trying since 1928, it had been some wait.

If rugby followers thought France's brilliance in 1997 and 1998 heralded the potential for a wonderful attacking World Cup of 1999, hosted by Wales, they were sadly deluding themselves.

It was a tournament of largely boring predictability, lit up only really by one match, the semi-final at Twickenham between New Zealand and France. The All Blacks seemed in complete control until a sudden second-half French storm which produced four tries in little more than twelve minutes, turned the game on its head. From a comfortable lead, the All Blacks found themselves swept away to a 43-31 defeat. Alas, that was about it as far as the thrills went.

France couldn't repeat their brilliance in the final against a superbly organised Australian defence that strangled the life out of every opponent. Coached by Rod Macqueen, the Wallabies won a disappointing final and a somewhat flat event, 35 points to 12. The eleven penalty goals somehow epitomized most of the tournament.

David Campese
Australia 1982–1996
Wing

A mercurial character who enjoyed flouting convention and played his rugby in similar style. Won 101 caps for Australia between 1982 and 1996 and established a reputation as the most exciting, entertaining player of his generation. He remains far and away Australia's record try scorer with sixty-four tries in his century of Tests.

'Coming from a small town in Australia, where I grew up surrounded by rugby league, I just played for fun. And I tried to follow that approach throughout my career. Mind you, it was different in those days to the present time. When we went on tours in the 1980s, we had some doctors and lawyers amongst us and a few were even doing exams or preparing for them at the airports. That was why rugby was somehow more than just about sport. It was a lot more prestigious.

The Wallabies 1984 Grand Slam tour of Britain and Ireland was really special. We had a coach in Alan Jones who was ahead of his time and that was another of the reasons we won the Grand Slam. Jones was a disciplinarian and if you wanted to be in the team, you had to play to what he wanted. He would give you the info about people and expect you to deliver. But we also had some fantastic players, and they were vital. You can be the world's greatest coach but if you haven't got the players to work with, you won't win.

People in Britain and Ireland just enjoyed rugby, that was all, and we played the sort of rugby they wanted to see. They probably hadn't seen the skills we showed compared to what they were used to.

That tour was also an opportunity to travel the world and see new places. I never thought I would play rugby at the highest level or go to all those places so to be given the honour and privilege of touring with Australia was something else as far as I was concerned. I would have gone anywhere to play rugby. I just loved the game.

That tour was great because we met so many different people. And when you go back years later, you see some of them again and enjoy the friendships once

Opposite: The brilliantly gifted 'Campo' began with ACT but moved to Sydney, where he played alongside the skilful Ella brothers for Randwick and NSW.

David Campese

more. To me, that was what rugby was about. Now, it's just a job for these guys; it's not what it was. And the modern players won't meet people and have a drink with them.

I found it very character building to play for the Wallabies at destinations all over the world. When you played in a provincial country town in New Zealand on a Wednesday afternoon or at Llanelli or Swansea on a Saturday, you learned so much. I came into the Wallabies side at 19 and just listened and learned. That way, you acquire the knowledge that enables you to set examples to the next generation.

It was tough at times; you had to work and train hard. But we looked forward to training then; now, it's just a job for the modern players, that's all they have to do. The Wallaby teams of that time also had a lot of leaders and that is something that has changed compared to now. You haven't got any leaders much today. But the more leaders on the field, the better team you will have.

The 1988 Australian tour of the UK wasn't as successful for the team but for me personally, it was a good one. 1988 was my best season and I played well. I felt good, felt fit and didn't have too many worries in my life. We had toured New Zealand in 1986 and won there at last, but in 1987 we failed to win the World Cup at home and copped a lot of criticism. When we came away in 1988, there wasn't as much pressure on that UK tour.

We won the World Cup in 1991 which was a fantastic thing for us. But in 1995 in South Africa, a lot went wrong. I'd gone from 82 kg to 92 and those 10 kg I put on, meant I lost a lot of my speed. Sure, I'd added bulk but lost pace. That was down to Bob Dwyer trying to get big guys in his team. But we also had four of the pack injured, that didn't help. South Africa caught us on the hop at the start of that 1995 World Cup and things had started to change. Not for the better either, in many ways.

After the game against England, Nick Farr-Jones, who was the senior player, said to George Gregan, "Come to my room and we'll talk". But Gregan never even turned up. That showed the arrogance of people and the problems we had off the field. Guys were worrying more about what was happening off the field than with the actual game. If it had been me, I'd have been the first one there in those circumstances because I wanted to learn and improve.

Professionalism was coming way back in the first half of the 1980s. I played in Italy from 1984 to 1992 and I was in effect a professional. But my attitude never changed. I just wanted to play rugby. I was there because I enjoyed rugby and my goal was to be the best possible player in my position. Sure, the Italians looked after me. But money wasn't my No. 1 target. How could it have been? I used to turn up for Barbarians games over Christmas at Leicester and stand around for hours after signing autographs. I never minded; it was always great to play. But you wouldn't get players doing that now. When the Barbarians play these days, the players get £5,000 each. And they play rubbish rugby.

I continue to believe that even now, if you had a player who combined work with his rugby, he would be a lot better as a player because he would have more things on his mind than just rugby. Unless you are really dedicated not just to be a player but to be the best player in the world in your position and your mind is fresh and focused, then a mixture of professionalism and amateurism would probably suit most guys.

To me, being a professional player is not about money, but attitude. If you haven't got the attitude, it doesn't matter how much money they give you. The best players have always had the best attitude. What was it Gary Player said, "It's a strange thing but the harder I practise, the better I get."

'I never quite knew where my legs were going.' David Campese in action against the Barbarians in 1984.

François Pienaar
South Africa 1993–96
Flanker

François Pienaar had a comparatively short international career for South Africa, from only 1993–96, but he was captain for every one of his 29 caps and is best known for being an inspirational leader and captaining the Springboks to the 1995 World Cup.

'There can be no better feeling for a rugby player than to win the Rugby World Cup. But perhaps in a wider sense there can be a more important element attached to that achievement. The feeling was that our nation came together in the light of that World Cup and South Africa's triumph for the first time in total harmony and rejoicing. By anybody's standards, that was some success in an altogether wider context than just rugby football.

Yet when South Africa was readmitted to international rugby in 1992 after the years of isolation, I felt the task confronting us was immense. We quickly had to learn about international rugby again. We were still quite competitive in terms of pure rugby playing despite isolation, because of our competitive Currie Cup programme. Yet we soon found out what the apartheid era had cost us in a rugby sense when we went out into the wider world and played on that stage. The truth was, we were well behind the other countries.

Therefore, we had to catch up and learn and we did that rather quickly. But then, we had to; we were staging the World Cup just three years later. So much expectation existed within our country regarding that tournament.

In the absence of international rugby, the game in the provincial arena within South Africa had become almost tribal with provinces playing each other in front of 50,000 crowds. But then, once we were readmitted, South African rugby had new horizons to pursue, starting with the southern hemisphere's Super 10 tournament in 1993. Transvaal, the team I captained, did very well and beat Auckland 20-17 in the final. Some key players, such as Pieter Hendriks, Japie Mulder, Hennie Le Roux, Balie Swart, Kobus Wiese and myself would go on to play in the World Cup final two years later.

The following year, 1994, Natal reached the final of the Super 10 tournament before going down 21-10 to Queensland in Durban. It meant a lot of our

François Pienaar

leading players were gaining much needed experience from that. We needed to play international rugby, to go overseas again and encounter the difficulties of that process. It also gave us an insight into the standards that existed in New Zealand and Australia, both of which countries were sure to be leading contenders for the 1995 World Cup.

In 1994, I went on my first major tour to that part of the world for a three-match Test series against New Zealand. It was a very tough tour with a lot of controversies and we lost it, 2-0 with the third Test drawn 18-all. But for me, the most valuable factor was the incredibly steep learning curve we were still engaged upon. It gave me much food for thought and the draw in the final Test, a match we were unlucky not to win, provided a nice platform on which to build.

By the time 1995 arrived, I knew we would be a young team going into what was an extremely important tournament for the whole of South Africa. I did not minimize the value of the event in any sense. It is not necessary to go through all the fine details of that World Cup here: everybody knows what happened. But suffice to say, South Africa were not the favourites going into that World Cup, Australia were. In my mind, they were an unbelievable team. Therefore, to upset them in the first game was very important. After that, there was always the belief in my mind that we could go all the way and so it turned out. But of course, finals are always tough and they can come down to just one missed tackle or one successful kick.

It was an incredibly emotional experience at the final whistle in that 1995 final, although I never rejoiced openly after a win. It was only really later that I got the whole picture as to what it actually meant to the entire country.

And even today, twelve years later, when I drive around South Africa, people still recognize me and still talk about that day and what it meant for the country. It was a special moment and we had our place in the sun.

And what of our legacy? It is not for me to say whether the legacy has matched that achievement. But I would have to say, look at the curve in the last ten years and it has not been a great trend compared to the other countries. That is disappointing for we have the talent definitely to be in the top three in the world, if not the top two.

One reason for that is, the outstanding team that had won the World Cup, was dismantled prematurely. South Africa was just starting to play the type of rugby that could have led the world game. We had a massive performance against England at Twickenham at the end of 1995, beating them 24-14. But breaking it up too soon meant that side never really peaked.

Something else I should say is that professionals had destroyed South African rugby for a long period. That spell of professionalism was badly managed and I include the players in that criticism. To my mind, no-one in South African rugby has yet grasped the concept of professional rugby and what it really means. It is not about money, it is about being professional in the way you behave, what you do, how seriously you take your work, how you prepare yourself for training, matches or the organization of the game.

As for the future for the game in South Africa, I believe we can anticipate a great era. We have seen in the last couple of years stars coming through and their achievements have grabbed the imagination of the world. I just hope for the sake of rugby in South Africa that those star players will be able to realize their full potential.

For the fact is, I still love this game and always will do. And my feelings are shared by countless numbers of people in the new South Africa.

,

'It was an incredibly emotional experience at the final whistle in that 1995 final'. The usually reticent Pienaar raises his arms in triumph as South Africa win the Webb Ellis trophy on their first attempt and on home soil.

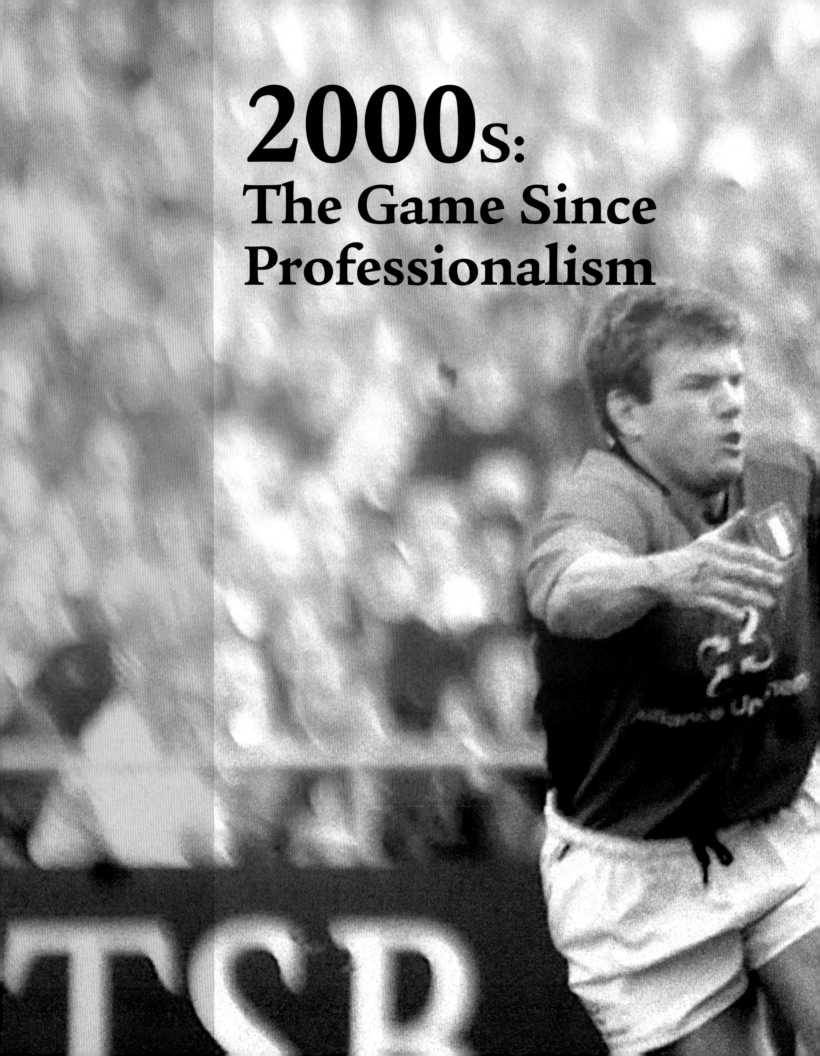

2000s:
The Game Since Professionalism

2000s: The Game Since Professionalism

Given the fact that New Zealand's population is still not many more than three million, you have to admire the way their country has harnessed to the utmost advantage the rugby players they do have. Their hunger, drive and determination, not to mention their excellence and technical proficiency know no limits.

Hand on heart, name the greatest rugby nation of the last sixty years. Well, a few might have pretensions to the title. France has contributed hugely to the world game with its unique brand of colour, noise, invention, power and panache. South Africans have been proud, mighty warriors and won a magnificent World Cup, largely against the odds in 1995.

But then, if winning the World Cup is your criteria, how about Australia, who remained at the start of 2007, the only nation to have lifted the coveted William Webb Ellis trophy twice? Given its comparatively small playing base, Australia has done marvellously over the course of the last twenty-five years in making its considerable mark upon the world rugby scene. With characteristic guts and endeavour, the Wallabies have become a feared side around the world. At their best, they are strong, resourceful and inventive. Above all, they have men who intrinsically know and understand the game. The latest example is Michael Foley, assistant to John Connolly at the 2007 Rugby World Cup, together with Scott Johnston. Foley, who himself played in the 1999 World Cup final as the Australian hooker, is one for the future, a quietly determined, knowledgeable rugby man. In the hands of people like this, Australian rugby is bound to go forward.

Nor should we forget Wales, that geographically small land tucked on the western edges of the British Isles but a handsome contributor to the pantheon of rugby gods, with the likes of Cliff Morgan, Barry John, David Watkins, Gareth Edwards, Mervyn and Gerald Davies, J. P. R. Williams and so many more.

But for my money, there is a clear winner. It has to be New Zealand. Sustained excellence must be the critical yardstick in any such debate and New Zealand has achieved that in every decade of the last half century.

It could be argued that the All Blacks failed by their own high standards, in four successive World Cups, but this was only due to some rare, spectacularly successful one-off performances which denied them in those tournaments. That does not alter the reality.

By every measure, surely, this country merits the title 'Greatest rugby nation of the last sixty years'. Names like Whineray, Meads, Lochore, Mourie, Gray, Nathan, Leslie, Clarke, Fitzpatrick, Lomu, Gallagher, Haden, Bunce, Whetton, Fox, Kirk, Loveridge, Kirwan, Mehrtens, Marshall, Wilson, Randell, Dalton, Jones, Brooke, McCaw, Carter and legions more command a respect that is universal. For me, New Zealand stands alone as the nation that defines the game: hard, tough and as fiercely competitive on the field as warm, welcoming and wonderfully hospitable,

Previous pages: Ireland's Brian O'Driscoll breaks through the Italian line.

Opposite: Dan Carter demonstrates his raw power as it takes two French defenders to slow him.

off it. It is a heady combination as befits the greatest rugby nation on earth.

Enjoyment and knowledge of the game is a passport to lifelong friendships with the people of New Zealand. They are an utterly singular people, perhaps at times incapable of removing the blinkers and seeing a wider picture. Their geographical isolation down at the bottom of the world is partly responsible for that but it is hardly a hanging offence.

In rugby terms, and in the field of consistency, they have had few equals these last sixty years and those challengers who have stood up against them successfully have invariably not sustained their excellence.

A Sleeping Giant Stirs

In the early years of the new millennium, New Zealand and England stood out as the two countries that had dominated the world scene.

The growing seeds of England's ascendancy began, ironically enough, with the controversial decision to leave Clive Woodward in charge despite England's defeat in the quarter-finals of the 1999 World Cup. On a bizarre day in Paris, the South African outside-half Jannie de Beer dropped an extraordinary five goals to help see off England's challenge 44-21.

These days, such a thrashing would almost certainly have led to the replacement of the coach and despite some hysterical calls for Woodward's head, he was retained. It proved to be a decision of absolutely critical importance.

Woodward set about rebuilding England and he demanded the Rugby Football Union provide every possible assistance. It is said the RFU spent around £8 million on England's World Cup preparations for 2003. Under Woodward's meticulous eye, not a thing was left to chance, not an opportunity for excellence was overlooked. There was a zealous determination to prepare assiduously and every single aspect of that preparation was minutely scrutinized. If errors were seen, they were addressed there and then. In terms of practice on the training ground, the move would be repeated time and time again until it was perfect. This dedication to perfection was at the heart of England's eventual supremacy.

The team was rebuilt around a core of experienced, world-class performers and those who joined them had myriad talents of their own to contribute.

Men like the venerable Martin Johnson, as natural a leader as Churchill, provided the solid ballast. Others, like Lawrence Dallaglio, Phil Vickery, Neil Back, Richard Hill and Steve Thompson offered qualities of their own.

Behind the scrum, there was the brilliantly gifted Jonny Wilkinson, a goal kicker of metronomic consistency. Outside him, Will Greenwood was a true footballer down to his cotton socks and his skills were the ideal foil to the more physical efforts of players like Mike Tindall and Ben Cohen. Finally, there was the former rugby league star Jason Robinson, an elusive, jinking runner who could stand up an opponent and skip past him in space as limited as a phone box.

This heady combination, with the assistance of others in the team and squad, took England to the summit of the world game. But the greatest irony was that by the time they went to Australia for the 2003 Rugby World Cup, they had clearly peaked and were past their best.

Performances that qualified as the defining moments of England's excellence in the first three years of the 2000s were plentiful. England were Six Nations Champions in 2000 and 2001, and in those years they achieved some extraordinary results. In 2000, Ireland were humiliated 50-18 at Twickenham, Wales suffering a similar humbling with a 46-12 defeat. England won in Paris and Rome, too, but messed up the Grand Slam by slipping and sliding their way to a 19-13 upset in poor conditions against the marvellously feisty Scots at Murrayfield. It wasn't the first time Englishmen had been sent home disappointed by their northern neighbours.

No matter, the rugby played under the inspirational back-line coaching of Brian Ashton, who was to return as senior coach at the end of 2006 when Andy Robinson departed, was magnificent. There was a style, an élan to England's rugby that buried memories of their traditional forward-orientated play. Suddenly, it was as though the shackles had at last been cast aside.

One of England's finest ever forwards: Lawrence Dallaglio.

Following pages: At the end of a remarkable game, the final whistle sparks English celebrations.

Jonny Wilkinson drops the winning goal and then reels away in celebration (*opposite*) in the dying seconds of the 2003 Rugby World Cup as England become the first northern hemisphere team to win the William Webb Ellis trophy.

In 2001, there was the extraordinary sight of France being put to the sword at Twickenham in a 48-19 thrashing. England's superiority was so obvious that they ran up 80 points against Italy, 44 in Cardiff against Wales and 43 against Scotland at Twickenham. But again, a flaw was detected: they lost 20-14 to Ireland in Dublin and another Grand Slam went out of the window.

All those obvious highlights were exceptional displays. But if there was one match that epitomized England's steely resolve to achieve, their ability in this era to take on the best and beat them whatever the circumstances or surroundings, it had to be the match against New Zealand at Wellington in 2003. There never can be excuses when you play New Zealand: for every nation, it is judgement day. You either stand tall and perform or succumb.

At one point in that game, England were reduced to thirteen men after two players had been sent to the sin bin. But they then withstood the fury and might of a full New Zealand side, resisting the will of the All Blacks in their own backyard with as commendable a display of character, guts and sheer will, as you could ever see. England eventually won that match 15-13, and it defined them as the best team in the world at that time. One week later, they earned a comprehensive 25-14 win over Australia in Melbourne, to confirm the point.

True, there had been those slips, those days when, as Martin Johnson was to say later, 'we tried to play too much rugby'. In 2002, France beat them in Paris to win the Grand Slam. But England's 53-3 annihilation of South Africa at Twickenham later that year, a match of such physical brutality and mental anguish for the South Africans that their captain Corné Krige was in tears at the pain and humiliation in the dressing room afterwards, underlined England's eminence.

They carried that ascendancy into the 2003 World Cup. Ultimately, it proved enough, but only because England had such a leader in Johnson. Late in normal time, after English fumblings and hesitancy had squandered the opportunity to put an inferior Australian side to the sword much earlier in the final, Johnson stood tall. In the moments before extra time began, the scores locked at 14-14 after eighty minutes, Johnson calmly told his team, 'We have done more than enough to win this World Cup, it should be over. Now let's go and finish the job.'

They did, but only after the England captain had steadied his team's growing nerves, taking responsibility and winning crucial line-outs at vital moments. Wilkinson's drop goal then finally nailed the Wallabies and England were into the record books for ever. Frankly, they deserved it.

It was vindication for the RFU's backing for Woodward in the light of England's 1999 failure and, ironically, confirmation that the best had been seen of this great England side. The truth was, it had been at its zenith more than a year before yet had still been good enough to hang on through to the World

Cup the following October and win it. Only special teams can achieve such feats.

In the wake of England's inevitable demise (caused by the loss of key men like Johnson, Wilkinson, Hill and Back), other countries took up the mantle.

In 2000, France played a home Test series against New Zealand. The French lost the first Test in Paris 39-26 but squared the series with a powerful performance in the second Test at Marseille, winning 42-33. It was a reminder to the All Blacks that the French were dangerous, just as they had been in coming so gloriously from behind to topple the All Blacks in the second half of the 1999 Rugby World Cup semi-final at Twickenham.

The French enjoyed some significant successes in the first half of the 2000s. They won a Grand Slam in the Six Nations Championship in 2002 and 2004 as well as ending up Champions in 2006 and 2007. They overwhelmed most opponents, beating Scotland in six successive meetings in the Championship, including a 38-3 hammering in Paris in 2003. No surprise, then, that when the two countries met in the World Cup later that year, France won 51-9 and followed it up with a 31-0 hiding at Murrayfield in the Six Nations the following winter.

England inflicted similar humiliations on the hapless Scots, scoring 43, 29, 40, 35 and 43 points against them from 2001 to 2005. Encouragingly for the Scots, however, the arrival of Frank Hadden as coach in time for the 2006 Six Nations brought better results. Both France and England were beaten at Murrayfield in 2006, much needed wins for a nation that is struggling badly to stay in touch with the leading rugby countries of the world. Scotland's player base is much reduced, interest likewise. It is a disturbing trend in a land that has produced some outstanding players of world-class talent down the years. A wooden spoon in 2007 did not ease concerns.

The embers of traditional fire in the other Celtic nations have been more obvious. A long awaited Grand Slam for Wales in 2005, their first for twenty-seven years, was greeted with raucous acclaim throughout the principality. Welsh rugby had known some tough times in that intervening period, but to see the enthusiasm, the passion and interest come once more to life in a manner that perhaps only the Welsh can demonstrate, was to experience a marvellous sensation. Injuries and internal dissent, which culminated in the departure of coach Mike Ruddock, then combined in classically Welsh style to bring them crashing down to earth in 2006. The 2007 similarly contained many disappointments.

But under the shrewd guidance of another excellent man of rugby, Gareth Jenkins, it is to be hoped that Wales will make progress. European and indeed world rugby needs them at their feisty, talented best.

As for Ireland, they went into 2007, World Cup year, as the most obviously talented side in Europe. Triple Crowns in 2004, 2006 and 2007, as well as four successive victories over England in 2004, 2005, 2006 and 2007 plus defeats of South Africa and Australia in November 2006, emphasized their progress.

The Irish also enjoy wise counsel from an astute coach, Eddie O'Sullivan. But they have world-class talents in players like Gordon D'Arcy, Brian O'Driscoll and Paul O'Connell. Now, though, they have found more players of proper international

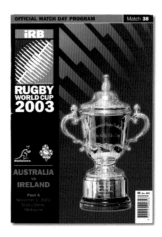

The programme for the 2003 Australia v Ireland World Cup game.

Opposite: Brian O'Driscoll breaks through the Australian defence during their match at Lansdowne Road in November 2006. Ronan O'Gara scored 11 points for Ireland in a 21-6 win over Australia.

ability to enhance the overall strength. Perhaps Ireland's greatest challenge will be to continue to unearth players of excellence. Without them, the path trodden by Scotland is one the Irish might come to fear with their limited playing numbers.

In 2004, when New Zealand returned to France, it was the French who received a rugby lesson. The All Blacks smashed them aside 45-6 in Paris, with a performance of blistering power, physicality and penetration. It showed the world that a new era had begun for New Zealand and not a side in the world would be allowed to dictate to them.

New Zealand was the southern hemisphere's Tri-Nations champions in 2002 and 2003, following two years of Australian ascendancy. True, in 2004, a revitalized South African side, inspired by their new coach Jake White, won the competition. But like so many others, the South African ascendancy was merely temporary. England's had been likewise; magnificent in its pomp, but not sufficiently long lasting to merit acclaim as the best of a decade or, still less, half a century.

Take the Tri-Nations tournament since its inception in 1996 through to 2006. Both Australia and South Africa have won it twice each. New Zealand has done so seven times in those eleven seasons. This consistency is what has defined New Zealand rugby over the last sixty years.

And after the ignominy of 2004, New Zealand came again. True, they needed a late try by their impressive hooker Keven Mealamu to pip the South Africans at the end of their Tri-Nations Test in Dunedin the following year. But they followed that 2005 southern hemisphere conquest with a repeat dose in 2006. The only difference was that the New Zealand aura of invincibility was growing.

The arrival of Graham Henry as coach, with the experienced former Wales coach Steve Hansen and ex-All Blacks coach Wayne Smith as his assistants plus All Black great Sir Brian Lochore as senior selector, gave New Zealand a rugby brains trust of formidable proportions.

Joe Rokocoko heads for the try line during the All Blacks record-breaking 50-21 win over Australia in Sydney in the 2003 Tri-Nations.

In 2006, New Zealand embarked upon an impressive European tour. The French were wiped off the field in Lyon in a first Test so one-sided it brought shame and humiliation to the locals. New Zealand won 47-3 and left not the slightest vestige of doubt that they enjoyed an overwhelming psychological advantage over their humbled opponents.

The second Test in Paris was closer, yet New Zealand, even though far from their best, finished clear 23-11 winners. French rugby had been silenced. There was none of the traditional French forward fire, spirit shown by players not prepared to bow the knee to any opponent. Behind the scrum, meanwhile, France seemed also to have lost the intuitive brilliance of her three-quarters. Those off-the-cuff skills had lit up world rugby through the years, but suddenly, French rugby seemed somehow formulaic, predictable. For sure, it was cleaner and the villains had been expunged from the scene. But so much of the French character had gone with them. Frankly, it left them looking like half the team they once were, and the 2007 Six Nations title, which they clinched on the final day of the season, did nothing to dispel that impression.

In late 2006, England at Twickenham and Wales at Cardiff, the latter by 45 points to 10, likewise fell beneath the wheels of the New Zealand chariot. It seemed unstoppable.

Frank Bunce was an All Black of quality. He won 55 caps for them as a centre from 1990–97, following four at the start of his career for Samoa. He played for New Zealand in the 1995 World Cup final against South Africa in Johannesburg and is philosophical with regard to All Blacks not having won a World Cup for over 20 years.

'The long held appetite in our country to become an All Black is as strong as ever. That has never diminished ...'

'We virtually surrendered in 1999 to France. I think in 1995, we could be forgiven because we did just about everything except win. We reached the final and most people said we played the best rugby. But that's the way tournaments can go, anyone can beat anyone on the day.'

Bunce went on, 'The long held appetite in our country to become an All Black is as strong as ever. That has never diminished. Professional rugby players sometimes get criticised after a bad performance for only being in the game for the money, but the truth is in New Zealand, the fire and desire to be an All Black still burns as fiercely as it ever did. You want to do the best for that jersey. Another factor is, I think we have an inherent advantage. We have a lot of natural skill and ball talent in our country. Perhaps it's the influence of the Maoris and Pacific island families but other countries don't have that. A lot of these people can do things with a ball without any training. Plus, we are an outdoors nation. All these things give us a little bit of an edge.'

But not everything New Zealand rugby does and in which it is involved, is commendable. One of the greatest disappointments of the 2000s was to see Argentina still unable to break into the upper echelons of the world game on a consistent basis. Their playing record was easily good enough to justify higher playing levels. Indeed, from 2002 to 2004, they beat France four times in succession before France scrambled to a single-point victory in late 2006 and by the start of the decade,

Following pages: New Zealand's Carlos Spencer runs the ball past Juan Smith and Joost van der Westhuizen during the All Blacks' 19-11 win over the Springboks in the Tri-Nations Test at Dunedin in 2003.

Argentina had carved out a compelling case for inclusion in the southern hemisphere's Tri-Nations Championship. They proved an increasingly tough assignment for any nation, especially in Buenos Aires. Their presence in a lopsided Tri-Nations tournament that forced South Africa to suffer much the worst of the travel schedule would have greatly enhanced the event and levelled out the travelling commitment. But the reaction of New Zealand, Australia and South Africa was one of reluctance. As yet these great rugby playing nations have still to extend a hand of friendship, eager to help a burgeoning rugby nation expand its horizons and improve its fortunes on the world stage, nor have they encouraged the development of the game in South America by offering them a share of the revenue that the Tri-Nations generates.

Even into the second half of the new millennium's first decade, Argentina were still left scrabbling for crumbs discarded by the masters at their table. All they got was the occasional visit from one of their fellow southern hemisphere teams to Buenos Aires. In the last seventeen years, Australia has only been to Argentina twice, New Zealand likewise in fifteen years. Admittedly, the South Africans have been better friends, visiting five times in fourteen years.

For Argentine rugby to grow sufficiently so as to provide a reliable, competitive opponent for the best teams in the game, the Pumas must be given a place in a major competition. If this invitation is again refused when the next southern hemisphere TV deal is brokered, things may change. The new South African rugby union president Oregan Hoskins has already indicated the Springboks would be better off in an expanded Six Nations tournament based in Europe.

Opposite: Mirco Bergamasco looks for support from team-mate Matteo Pratichetti. Italy triumphed in two consecutive 2007 Six Nations matches for the very first time, showing that they are no longer the walkovers they were once seen to be.

Argentina's elegant full-back Juan Martin Hernàndez scores a try against France in November 2006. France won 27-26 but the close score demonstrated the great strides that Argentina, one of the so-called lesser rugby-playing nations, was making.

If the Six Nations organizers were smart, they would welcome them with open arms, together with Argentina, who could play their 'home' matches in Barcelona or Madrid. The acquisition of those two nations would make a new, Eight Nations tournament by far the best in the world.

The magical lure of the old Five Nations Championship was always the trips it offered to destinations like Cardiff, Dublin, Edinburgh, London and Paris. Add on Barcelona or Madrid, then factor in a trip to a city like Cape Town for one of the Springboks home games and the tournament would be the envy of the sporting world. Its value to television would be enormous.

What such a dramatic reconfiguration of the world rugby map might also do is force New Zealand and Australia to bring the likes of Japan, Fiji and

A night to remember. Ireland made history by welcoming England to historic Croke Park and then re-writing the record books by thumping them 43-13 in February 2007.

Samoa into a new competition in their part of the world.

We live now in an age where most of the old customs and traditions are being discarded. Whether that is a good or bad thing is entirely a different issue. What it does mean for certain is that fresh, lateral thinking is required. Scenarios never before envisaged can now be contemplated quite openly, as long as the finances stand up. And in that field, television is and will remain the master. TV will always buy into what it perceives as 'sexy' events, tournaments with a cachet, an appeal.

Manifestly, an Eight Nations tournament including South Africa and Argentina would make for exceptional viewing and huge interest. Every country involved could expect to enhance its product and its finances. It might not suit some countries in the southern hemisphere like New Zealand and Australia. But their intransigence and delay in denying Argentina a place at the top table has opened up the possibility of such a situation unfolding towards the end of the 2000s.

However, that fear of isolation will, I believe, force New Zealand and Australia to accept Argentina's entry into the next southern hemisphere Tri-Nations TV deal, especially if, as seems likely, South Africa are continuing to make noises about abandoning the Tri-Nations. Such a threat has frightened Australia and New Zealand.

Perhaps the chief task for rugby union in the last years of this decade is how to ensure the game grows in countries like Japan. As the centre of Asia in terms of business and so many other activities, Japan has to be the flag carrier of the game in the coming years. China, with its phenomenal growth, is very like the United States of America in this sense: both remain only a figment of most people's imagination in terms of becoming world powers in rugby union any time soon.

Unfortunately, the people who run the International Rugby Board seem not understand this key point. Their decision to reject Japan's bid to stage the 2011 Rugby World Cup was a tragedy for the game, a decision that in the coming years will increasingly be seen as a huge missed opportunity for the future of the sport.

If the game is to grow exponentially in the remainder of the 2000s and then into the next decade of the 21st century, it has to embrace change and new horizons in a far more positive manner. Japan, if it bids again, must be awarded the 2015 World Cup. Keeping the tournament exclusively in the traditional rugby-playing nations has gone on too long.

Proof that the game can move forward and overcome obstacles came in spring 2007 when England travelled to play Ireland at Croke Park for the very first time.

Just a peep at the history behind this emotive fixture was sufficient to understand the surging emotions felt by every Irishman. But Ireland's growing maturity as a nation was reflected in the immaculate way the English national anthem was received. It spoke volumes for the warm welcome always associated with the Irish and was testimony to their fair mindedness. And the pumping adrenalin felt by every Irish player was borne out by their annihilation of England, a 43-13 win that was one of their finest performances in years. For sure, it owed much to their skills as fine players. But it also revealed the power of passion within any sport. Ireland were so fired up that night hardly a team in the world could have lived with them.

Martin Johnson
England 1993–2003
Lock Forward

Martin Johnson led England to their greatest triumph, the 2003 Rugby World Cup which climaxed a magnificent career. He won 84 caps for England, making his debut against France in 1993 and ending with the World Cup final. At 2.01 m and 119 kg, Johnson was a powerful lock-forward and an inspiration with his quiet, firm leadership for Leicester and England.

'I played with so many fine players and was lucky enough to enjoy much success. I can hardly begin to say how fortunate I was.

Was England's World Cup winning side its' best team? After all, in 2001 we scored the most tries in the Six Nations Championship but we didn't win it.

To me, peaking is when you win the game. In 2003 we lost only one game, when we sent out ten reserves against France in Marseille. That was the best season.

Maybe we played the more entertaining rugby in the two years before that. But you cannot ignore results. In 2003, we won the Grand Slam and then beat New Zealand and Australia on a southern hemisphere tour, on consecutive weekends. That is the only time England has managed that. We couldn't have been in a much better position going into that World Cup.

We were a team better at winning those close games than we were the one-sided ones. When we lost to Ireland in 2001 in Dublin, we just tried to play too much rugby. Always remember, you have to win the game first. That still applies as much as ever; you must win first.

New Zealand today plays a high-pressure game and puts teams under a lot of pressure. That is what rugby is all about. We just did whatever we could to win the game. It is the sign of a good team whatever the conditions, whatever needs to be done you try and do it.

That summer tour to New Zealand and Australia in 2003 underlined that. We won the game in Wellington in conditions of pouring rain and mud, then the following week we played indoors against Australia in Melbourne and won again.

Opposite: 'There was never any doubt in my mind that we would win that final. Not even when we were held at the end of normal time.' Martin Johnson reflecting on England's 2003 World Cup triumph.

Martin Johnson

We played a completely different way in the second game but still won. That is the mark of a good team, when you can win in all circumstances and conditions.

What won the World Cup? The experience of the players? There was a lot more to it than that. A lot of effort and preparation by the coaches went into it and a lot of hard work by the players. People from outside try to see who or what was the decisive influence but it is difficult to be exact and put your finger on just who did what and how important that was to the overall achievement. But I would say Clive Woodward was always very much someone who could see the big picture and that was a major factor. He was clever and innovative. And he was desperately keen to be successful and win.

We had a lot of good players, of course, in terms of skills but they were hard workers too; their work ethic was second to none. We didn't have guys that got carried away when they won a match or two.

And with hindsight, maybe the fact that we had lost some crucial games along the way to the World Cup kept us hungry and focused. Maybe we wouldn't have been so determined had we won two or three Grand Slams on the trot in the Championship. Perhaps those results, like losing to Scotland in 2000, to Ireland in 2001 and to France in 2002, helped us keep a perspective.

When I look back, the satisfaction at our World Cup win comes from the fact that we matched the expectation put on us. We were the best team in the world and we justified that billing by ending up winners. We dealt with a lot too:
going away from home, dealing with the grief, the anti-Englishness you get, the fuss made over having sixteen players on the field against Samoa … things like that.

We had to try and handle all that stupid stuff and put it out of our minds. We overcame all that and kept concentrating on winning games. That factor gives me a lot of satisfaction.

Nor was there ever any doubt in my mind that we would win that final. Not even when we were held at the end of normal time. When we got into the huddle before extra time began, I looked in our guys' eyes and saw their body language. I saw their reaction to the thought of another test before us and I knew we were going to win. It's easy to say that now, but I honestly believed it at the time, too. I vividly remember looking at them and thinking to myself "We are going to win this game."

Australia had a good team but I felt that whatever they could have done, we would have matched them. Of course, we should have had the game won before then, we should have put it away in normal time. But we made mistakes; there were some refereeing decisions that were strange and other factors combined to prevent that. But you have to find a way past those difficulties and we did that.

The RFU also deserved credit for the part they played. They stuck with Clive Woodward after 1999 when so much of the media were demanding he be sacked.

For me it was always about just playing rugby. And the experiences we had when we were out in Australia kept things in perspective for us. The most pressurized game of that entire tournament for us was against South Africa in the pool match in Perth. The pressure was really on for that one, yet it was played against a backdrop of the wife of one of our players, Will Greenwood, being in danger of losing their child back in England. So you have to keep things in perspective: we were just playing a few games of rugby. How did they compare in importance to what Will and his wife were going through?

Rugby today is still a great sport with a huge amount of integrity. There are certain non-negotiable aspects contained within its charter. People said to me after the World Cup final, how did you keep your players from reacting against the referee? But this is rugby, you don't do those things. You don't argue with referees. There is a great integrity about the game and you strive to keep that.

When I look back on my career, I don't necessarily think about just the obvious highlights because your low points were also part of it all. That's life: you can't enjoy the high points if you haven't known low points as well. That is all part of your career, your life.

Martin Johnson can't contain his elation at final whistle of the 2003 World Cup final.

Mike Catt
England 1992–2007
Fly-half and Centre

A South African who came to England in 1992 to find a club where he could play a bit of rugby, Catt has won over sixty caps for England, with whom he shared World Cup and Grand Slam successes. A brilliantly creative midfield player, who has excelled at both fly-half and centre.

Being a player in these years has obviously been fantastic for me. In the first years of the 2000s, England played so well and we won the Grand Slam and then the World Cup. To achieve every goal I had ever dreamed of was superb from my point of view and I can always hold my hand up and say, "I did it all".

But from the point of view of the game's development, I have been very disappointed with the overall development of the players in the last four to five years. Not enough guys have come through that should have emerged.

In my view, they have spent too much time in the gym rather than working on skills. But you need those skills to be better than ever because defences are so well organized now. In New Zealand, it is different. Look at the New Zealand sides: everyone can pass, catch, run good lines and they're taking that into the Test arena. But we don't do it at international level in this country.

The whole coaching structure will have to change at club level because at the moment, everything is done as a team. But one-on-one coaching is vital and that is something I plan to do more of next year at my club, London Irish. We need to develop guys individually, giving each one half an hour most days so that they have the ability to progress as a player rather than just among a team where they can hide. You can't communicate those skills in a group.

It is not hard to rectify, it's having people that are capable of doing it, passing on their knowledge and getting players to understand the need for ball skills in the game. A lot of coaches are very good at organization but not many are good at one-on-one sessions. They don't understand what is required in that context. But this is where the younger generation of coaches that is coming through will have to be able to put this in force.

If you give these guys one-on-one coaching you can really get them working and doing it the right way. I want to give something back to the game and I have

Opposite: Mike Catt has won over 60 caps for England and captained the team in the second half of the 2007 Six Nations Championship.

Mike Catt

Mike Catt

already done a bit of this, whilst still a player. Rugby has been a brilliant part of my life and I am very fortunate still to be playing at 35 and enjoying myself. I have still got this drive and energy to want to continue to play.

The sport has gone forward so much, definitely. England winning the World Cup was a big moment and the coverage of rugby union has increased massively. In terms of crowd attendances, facilities and things put in place for players the game has been transformed over the last seven years or so. In England, there is a very physical and competitive club programme and that's been very healthy.

If agreement is reached over releasing players, it would do the game in England a hell of a lot of good. The club sides can still thrive but the international team would do much better. In the last few years since 2003 when we won the World Cup, the clubs have done well but the national team has struggled and you can't have that. We need both to succeed. The structure seems to work well in the southern hemisphere from the players' perspective. The size of these guys now is immense.

But the game has also become very structured with players being told where to go on the field and what to do rather than being allowed to do the instinctive things. That has been a massive negative side to professionalism. It has been too structured with not enough attention and focus on skills and decision-making.

I can't see how that is going to change in the short term because of the physicality and intensity of youngsters coming through now. So this is where I go back to the need for one-on-one coaching to get youngsters to learn and improve their core skills. When you see a youngster demonstrating those skills it is like a breath of fresh air.

Rugby union was always famous as a game for the capacity of players to do things off the cuff. They would see a situation in front of them and make a decision and I believe those qualities are still required, perhaps even more so in the modern game. But it hasn't always been like that in recent years. When I was still at Bath, the Australian coaches John Connolly and Michael Foley (now the coaches of Australia) came in and suddenly everything was very structured. We lost that individual flair because you weren't allowed to try things. That was very frustrating and quashed a lot of talent.

But long term, I do believe we will see more of this individualism again in the game. As long as the young guys coming through are not handcuffed mentally by an excessive structure, we can develop their skills and they can show their talents to the widest audiences. Surely that is what the game needs and wants.

I don't believe one side will dominate in the coming years of the professional era. Different teams will win in different seasons because it has become far more competitive nowadays. There might not be too many Grand Slams around in the years to come in the Six Nations.

Opposite: A brilliantly creative midfield player, Catt proved his worth to England both as a fly-half and centre.

The Future
of the Game

The Future of
the Game

Luxury new stadiums like the Stade de France, Paris, the Millennium Stadium, Cardiff, Australia's Telstra Stadium in Sydney, and Twickenham offer an image of rugby football that is at once dynamic and vibrant. Then there's the wonderful GAA ground at Croke Park, Dublin, where Ireland are playing their home games while Lansdowne Road is being redeveloped.

Almost invariably, when the host countries play a match in those venues, they sell out. The new Twickenham boasts an 82,000 capacity, Paris and Sydney 80,000 each, Cardiff 74,500. Big matches in these locations represent significant paydays for the Unions. In 2006, the English Rugby Union estimated that ticket sales would bring in approximately a quarter of the RFU's total £80 million revenue. Meanwhile, as 2007 began, Ireland started the demolition of their old Lansdowne Road ground in favour of a new luxury stadium, due for completion in 2009. By any standards, these are impressive achievements and figures. But they hide a worrying picture at the other end of the game.

> 'We just can't raise a team. We only have about ten players left at the club.'

Listen to a man like Geoff Upsdell, long-time servant of the English rugby club Osterley, on the outskirts of London. Osterley, founded in 1922, was a thriving junior club in the years of the 1960s, 1970s and 1980s. They ran eight teams each Saturday and the club was a throbbing hive of activity each week. Today, Osterley shares a ground with another local club, Old Isleworthians, out in the old Middlesex suburbs. But even that statement hides the terrible truth. Osterley Rugby Club is dying.

Upsdell, the club president, says, 'We just can't raise a team. We only have about ten players left at the club and they have to get a game in the Old Isleworthians side. I don't see Osterley surviving, we're existing in name only. Yet at one stage we were one of the best second-class clubs in the country.'

In the English county of Middlesex alone in the eleven years since professionalism, there has been a disturbing decline in interest and support for the junior game. Back in 1995, there were about 150 junior clubs in Middlesex. Today, that number has been slashed to just under seventy.

'There has been a huge reduction in the numbers who play rugby now. Some of our former players drifted away because they said they'd prefer to watch a professional game. In my day, you wouldn't dream of going to see clubs like Harlequins or Wasps play. You always preferred to play yourself,' said Upsdell.

Upsdell is one of those marvellous men who have served the game loyally all their lives. He joined the club in 1970, played for years at all levels and then helped out in myriad tasks and official positions. It saddens him to see his old club in this state, but as he says, it is a fate that has befallen so many.

Previous pages: New Zealand's Joe Rokocoko is stopped by the French defence in November 2006.

'The truth is, we're not surviving. We haven't put out a side this season, we haven't played as Osterley. We are still a club but we don't have a side. However, we're joining an ever-expanding group. The Centaurs club used to put out five or six sides each week – they no longer exist. Old Gaytonians fielded four or five teams regularly but lack of numbers there and at Old Kingsburians (who always had enough players for four teams) forced those two to merge as West London.

'Clubs who collectively used to put out ten or twelve teams each week have now banded together but they're struggling even to raise a single side. That's how bad it is.'

There are, says Upsdell, many reasons for this alarming state of affairs. Osterley used to attract a lot of their players from local schools but the decline in rugby in schools has meant that supply line has dried up. 'Schools don't play rugby around here anymore and everywhere, kids play less. Professionalism has just widened the divide between the top and the junior clubs.'

A Middlesex official admitted there had been widespread dismay and sadness at a recent meeting when Osterley's plight had been revealed. But he said, 'The biggest problems began when so many schools stopped playing rugby. This had a dramatic effect on the adult playing population. And to make matters worse, at many clubs now you can't find the officials to give voluntary time to administer the game.

'Another big difficulty is the number of kids who give up the game from 16 to 18. The RFU has had to recognize that among all the rugby-playing nations, the performance in England of governing the transformation from thousands

England's Josh Lewsey is wrapped up by Bruce Douglas and Ali Hogg of Scotland during the 2006 Six Nations Championship match between Scotland and England.

of kids playing mini rugby to junior club rugby, was the worst in the world. We are absolutely hopeless at it. When that problem was identified, the RFU focused resources on the clubs rather than the schools to keep the kids playing rugby. But that was a mistake.'

A sad one off case of an English junior club failing to adapt to the times, but of little concern to others? If only. Osterley's example is being mirrored throughout England as clubs of long standing suffer a significant reduction in playing numbers.

Whichever way you look at it, a full house of 82,000 at Twickenham with countless hospitality boxes stuffed full of people stuffing themselves and millions being taken by the RFU in a single day for TV rights, sponsorship and gate receipts, is just one side of English rugby. It is true that the English Rugby Union has spent many thousands of pounds trying to arrest this decline and in some areas and instances, has succeeded. But the general trend is disturbing at many traditional junior clubs.

Take Northern Ireland. There, former Ireland and Lions captain Willie John McBride reports a similarly worrying pattern. 'The game is in serious decline at junior level; the picture is one of concern. Even the Irish Rugby Football Union are beginning to show concern. Last year in Ulster alone, there were thirty-seven less teams playing the game.

'I know of several clubs that are struggling. One of them was my original club Randalstown. Antrim are also in difficulties and Derry, too; they're in terrible straits. They have had tough years, getting bombed out of their original home. They built a nice new clubhouse but they're struggling to keep the club afloat.'

But it isn't just the small junior clubs that have found life tough, says McBride. North of Ireland Football Club (NIFC) was the club of the great Jack Kyle, Noel Henderson and Mike Gibson. 'Imagine the history attached to that club,' says McBride. 'But it has gone, amalgamated with Collegians, the old pupils of Methodist College, as Belfast Harlequins. And at the end of 2006 they were struggling at the bottom of the All-Ireland League. It is very sad. When I played, those teams were mighty, proud teams.'

Much the same can be said in other countries, like Wales and Scotland, where numbers playing the game are decreasing. In Scotland, interest in the sport seems to be on the wane. At the end of 2006, a Magners Celtic League match was played between Glasgow Warriors and Edinburgh. It attracted a paltry, pathetic crowd of 2,613.

So how much of all this is attributable to the coming of professionalism? It is too easy to point the finger solely in that direction. When you analyse it, a wider problem can be detected, a point with which McBride concurs. The evolution of society in general with its wider array of interests and hobbies has reduced people's commitment to any one single activity, and rugby has not bucked this trend. Once thriving junior cricket clubs have similarly struggled or gone to the wall.

In the modern world, easier transport links offering travel to alluring destinations, an increasingly materialistic society in which financial accumulation has attained a far greater importance, not least to meet responsibilities, and the demands of

Opposite: A bloody Adrian Garvey after the third test match against the British and Irish Lions at Ellis Park in July 1997. South Africa won the match 35-16 but the Lions won the series 2-1.

families have all combined to damage any sporting activity's attraction. Young people in the computer age have rival interests, too.

It is certainly true of the modern-day man in his 20s or 30s, perhaps with the responsibility of a wife and young family. To find the time in his schedule to go training two nights a week for as much as eight or nine months of the year, plus play a match each weekend that may require him to be away from home for anything between eight and twelve hours, is increasingly impossible. Families are doing more together; thus, a husband keen on rugby might well go to watch a match, but perhaps take his wife with him. Then there is another element to consider: injuries.

The greater focus on physicality in the game has meant many young players have rejected the sport. In New Zealand, an increasing number of mothers expressed alarm at seeing their sons compete against youngsters of similar age from a background in the Pacific Islands, where young men grow physically bigger at a much younger age. This led to many New Zealand youngsters abandoning the game, either through their parents' wishes or their own decision.

Willie John McBride remembered, 'When I toured New Zealand with the Lions in 1971, one of my adopted schools was Wellington College. I would go and talk to the kids there when we played at Wellington. A couple of years ago, I went back to New Zealand and stayed with Colin Meads, one of my great old adversaries. We were talking about rugby in New Zealand and the schools and he told me that there were now soccer posts at Wellington College. Too many parents of the white boys told their sons, "You are not playing rugby any longer, it is too dangerous". When you have that kind of situation anywhere it is damaging for the game long term.'

> 'We were talking about rugby in New Zealand and the schools and he told me that there were now soccer posts at Wellington College.'

In France, happily, they report a five per cent increase in playing numbers in the last few years. There is little tradition of schools teaching the sport in the country. Youngsters wishing to take up the game join their local club at an early age and progress through the junior ranks to senior levels. Many of those clubs are subsidized by the local town. Yet we should do well to remember that soccer still attracts great swathes of young supporters in France.

In countries like Wales, Scotland and England, there has been a significant reduction in the actual numbers of schools playing the game. In many cases, soccer has replaced rugby. In England, where the large population of over 60 million has put great pressures on the need for houses, a lot of school playing fields have been sold off in the last twenty years. Undeniably, this has weakened rugby's base.

In Wales, rugby also suffered the effects of the old Grammar Schools dying out, centres of learning where masters were willing to give up some of their time out of hours to coach youngsters in the skills of the game. Great former Welsh internationals like Gareth Edwards tell you today that youngsters are more likely to have posters of Welsh soccer heroes like Ryan Giggs and Craig Bellamy on their walls than the latest Welsh outside-half or scrum-half.

In Argentina, enthusiasm in the sport has been maintained to an encouraging degree. Yet Les Cusworth, who was appointed Director of Rugby for the Argentine Rugby Union near the end of 2006, identified a problem known in so many other nations.

'How do we keep the 16- to 18-year-olds playing rugby?' he asks. 'That's a question not just being asked in Argentina but in England, Ireland, New Zealand ... everywhere. That is one of the challenges of my job, a real priority.'

A long way to go for an Englishman to find a new challenge? 'I love rugby and I love Argentina,' said Cusworth, who is married to an Argentinian. 'But this job is about the development of the game in that country.'

His role is to strengthen Argentine rugby and help move it, cautiously and carefully, towards the professional side of the game. It isn't as developed in a professional sense as in the British Isles, Ireland, France or in countries of the southern hemisphere like New Zealand, so work needs to be done on that front.

'They have been reluctant to take things forward. The old amateur game has been

France's Florian Fritz drives on to score the winning try against Wales in 2006 Six Nations.

the basis of the sport in the country. But they accept they must move forward and we will do that. There's a lot that needs to be done, a lot isn't right there' says Cusworth.

'But one of the key tasks is finding out why so many 16- to 18/19-year-olds give up the game. Argentina will always produce high-quality players because the sport is hugely popular. Each year, on the first weekend in November, as many as 1,500 players of the Under 18 and Under 20 age groups gather to play at a tournament in Mar del Plata. They travel immense distances from all over Argentina to be there. All that is testimony to their love of the game.

'But there is a wider question here and it is, what is happening to those 16- to 19-year-olds? So many are giving up the game and it doesn't matter which country you are talking about. We have to find out why that is.'

One of the reasons for the movement away from playing the sport is the growth of the TV culture. Television now offers such a glut of rugby from myriad countries that the supporter can find more than enough to satisfy his interest. He doesn't even have to leave his sitting room to see top-class rugby, not just from his own country but around the world. And TV's careful, professional packaging of the sport has, inevitably, brought a glitz, an aura to the top end of the game. With the focus on an allure of the elite, it was inevitable that plain and simple old junior club rugby would lose much of its appeal. By comparison, it has looked slow and outdated. Not cool, in modern parlance.

Yet there is an anomaly here. Interest in rugby union is surging worldwide. Ticket sales for the 2007 World Cup in France underline that point. It's just that playing numbers are declining in most countries at junior level. The problem is, as McBride points out, 'If the grassroots is dying, then it is only a question of time before the top level suffers too. I see my country Ireland struggling to get enough players in ten years time.'

Television has carefully adjusted kick-off times so as to maximize its worldwide audiences. Games in New Zealand now begin at 7.30 at night, early morning in the northern hemisphere. Yet the New Zealand authorities have found that attendances at the gate have suffered accordingly. People living in the country in a New Zealand winter won't go out and drive to cities like Christchurch, Wellington and Dunedin for a night-time kick-off. The costs of staying overnight make the visit prohibitively expensive, too.

In France, most internationals now do not start until 9 at night, an absurdly late hour for rugby followers but ideal for prime-time television viewers.

Thus, a tradition has been allowed to grow that rugby is a game that can be seen in your own sitting room. And by staying at home on match day, people can fit so many other things into their busy lives and schedules.

Addressing this imbalance may be vital to rugby's future. Television has been able to call the shots because it has paid the money the unions crave. But in 2006, a situation arose whereby the New Zealand authorities struggled to sell out their ground at Wellington, with its modest 36,000 capacity, for the Tri-Nations Championship match against South Africa. In Sydney two weeks later, there were as many as 20,000 unsold seats for the Test match against the Springboks. Alarm bells should ring loud and clear at such scenarios.

The loss of so many volunteer administrators from the amateur game when rugby went professional has been another matter of serious concern. So many of the countless numbers of men and women who gave so much of their spare time in the amateur era on a goodwill basis, seeking neither plaudits nor material rewards, drifted quietly away from the sport when rugby became professional. Their loss has been keenly felt, the world over.

McBride says, 'Rugby since professionalism has lost a lot of its volunteers and they were the ones who held rugby football together, certainly in Ireland. They encouraged people to play the game, gathered together lads in the vicinity, but those people are no longer involved with the game. Their loss has been substantial.'

Twelve years after professionalism arrived, some amateur clubs have despaired of replacing those lost workers and have hired paid staff to do some of the work. They see it as the only proper solution, even for clubs that remain amateur.

But the constant ebb and flow of the tides within society have also combined to damage rugby's old order. Around thirty or forty years ago, rugby clubs still offered

A new breed of All Blacks perform the haka prior to their Test match against France in November 2006 at the Stade de France.

The 'Pau Rocket' celebrates another try. French flyer Philippe Bernat-Salles was one of the most exciting players to light up world rugby during his international career spanning 1992–2001.

a valuable focal point for local communities. They were a social location, visited not just by those participating in the sport but others in the community who were welcomed to these friendly, lively venues for a Saturday night of fun and frivolity.

Of course, in those days, society was less sophisticated and the days of rugby men staying all evening at their clubhouse are long gone, which has meant that one of the age-old attractions of rugby clubs has diminished.

McBride believes those who made the original decision back in 1995 to plunge the sport without warning into the maelstrom of professionalism bear a heavy responsibility for its subsequent pains.

'They took the game into a professional world without any thought, planning or preparation. It was never thought through and the game has not recovered from that.'

Nevertheless, there have been advantages to the professional code. The sham that existed prior to the announcement in 1995 was ended forever, and a good thing too. Players receiving money under the counter, some vehemently denying payment when it was plainly apparent money was changing hands, allied to the general air of suspicion hardly befitted this game. In fact, it damaged it for too long.

At least the announcement brought these matters properly into the open. Players would be paid and would be free to demand a proper living wage for a full-time commitment to the sport.

True, the way things evolved have perhaps not been to everyone's liking. Players at the top level have become insulated from reality, sealed off from most supporters and critics. They drive to training in their sponsored cars, train behind closed doors, drive home again and play a match once a week. There is little fraternisation after games with supporters or opponents and the traditional banquets following internationals have largely died out. Professional players go straight into recovery sessions leaving no time for the old niceties and courtesies of the amateur sport. A pity perhaps, but that is the way of the modern world.

More seriously, the role of coaches has assumed an altogether greater importance. There are now head coaches, backs coaches, forwards coaches, defence coaches, attack coaches, skills coaches, hand/eye co-ordination coaches, fitness coaches, psychological coaches and more besides. This army of assistants, most of them paid full-time salaries, has swelled the wage bills of unions to grotesque levels. And, say some, what they have done is reduce the decision-making powers of the individual player almost to nil. Yet such individuality hallmarked the game.

Traditionally, rugby was played by people from a variety of backgrounds; those with great intellectual grey matter mingling with those who were just physically imposing or fast. Decisions would be made on the evidence in front of the player, not by some pre-programmed formula devised days or weeks earlier by the coach. Too much modern-day rugby suggests the latter; it is as though the game has become a giant, human chess game with pieces moved around the field according to situations, possession and territory. Surely, this is not how rugby union was meant to be played.

'When I played international rugby those 50,000 people in the stand were real rugby people but not now. The average rugby guy can't get tickets and couldn't afford to go even if he could.'

The best, the most inventive and exciting rugby was always played with a spark of inspiration and a large dash of the unexpected. Remember Gareth Edwards's famous try for the Barbarians against New Zealand in 1973 and the way it was started by Phil Bennett retreating towards his own line to collect a kick ahead. Who in the modern game would have the courage, the audacity to side-step out of defence the way Bennett did and then launch a movement that would end 90 metres upfield? It seems virtually inconceivable.

But rugby union at its vibrant best, its most aesthetically pleasing, always contained this element of unpredictability. Without it, games can seem bland and boring. Listen to Willie John McBride again.

'There is a hype about the game now and it has become very expensive. It is big entertainment but not rugby as I knew it. It is no longer a sport, it's huge entertainment geared largely to television and the corporate world. It's not geared to the true rugby guy.

'When I played international rugby those 50,000 people in the stand were real rugby people but not now. The average rugby guy can't get tickets and couldn't afford to go even if he could.'

Through professionalism, however, players have been able to work assiduously on their fitness. The modern-day international rugby player is so much faster and fitter than his predecessor in the old amateur era, as he should be. Imagine what a player like Gareth Edwards would have been like had he trained every day in a professional environment, without other preoccupations.

Medical advances and greater knowledge in the field of physical preparation and extracting the maximum performance from the body have also aided this rapid improvement in the physique and potential achievement of a top-class player. His injuries are analysed and treated immediately with the best professional care available. When fit, he is readied to perform at a level never known by the likes of Edwards and McBride.

But are we not entitled to ask, are the levels of decision-making any better than in an era of, say, the 1970s? In some cases, it seems doubtful. Plainly, the skill levels among the forwards have been transformed. Big men playing at prop or second row can now handle a ball and run in a manner never before envisaged. Their technique is infinitely superior. But behind the scrum, among the backs, the difference is less discernible.

Former 'greats' such as the Irishman Mike Gibson, Australia's Mark Ella, those mercurial Welsh fly-halves Cliff Morgan and Barry John, England's David Duckham, Gerald Davies of Wales or the great French centre Jo Maso were players of intuitive brilliance. The timing and their execution of skills allied to great vision and exemplary fingertip control of the ball meant they could unlock a defence with subtlety and cunning.

'There is a hype about the game now ... It is big entertainment but not rugby as I knew it.'

But how might they have handled the modern game? Without adding considerable bulk, they would scarcely have lasted in the ultra physical modern game with its lack of time and space. And what skills and speed might they have lost had they added significant weight? Even one of the world's greatest flair players, the former Australian wing David Campese, conceded that the decision to enhance his physique so that he went from 82 to 92 kg in time for the 1995 World Cup greatly reduced his speed and overall effectiveness.

In the modern game, physical bulk and power has become all. Thus, the game has evolved into something far closer to a battle of behemoths, a clash of physical giants more akin to American football or rugby league than the old amateur game of rugby union where skills were of the utmost importance. This is a shame, a matter of deep regret. But perhaps these so-called battles of behemoths provide a spectacle to the taste of modern audiences. By and large, rugby union crowds of former days were altogether more knowledgeable, more appreciative of the game's finer skills, its intricacies and subtleties than modern day audiences. But as Willie John McBride says, the composition of crowds at international matches has changed significantly. The corporate world has taken over these occasions, to the growing exclusion of the true rugby supporter.

What can we expect in the future? More of the same? If that proves to be so,

Opposite: Australian lock Justin Harrison celebrates after the Rugby World Cup semi-final match between Australia and New Zealand in November 2003. Australia beat New Zealand 22 points to 10.

then the careers of the leading players will become even shorter. Serious injuries are now an everyday occurrence for those at the top of the game, and size alone is no defence against them. Players of such physical magnitude primed to generate a pace never before within their capacity, have become explosive bundles of human danger, both to themselves and any opponents in the way.

By the start of 2007, the game worldwide was engaged in deep studies of these growing numbers of injuries and their implication for the sport of the future. For example, the International Rugby Board introduced a new procedure at the scrummage, aimed at eliminating the serious risk of major injury to front-row forwards at the engagement. It proposed carefully managed contact, hoping to avoid the crash of bodies hitherto seen as an integral part of the sport. The game's lawmakers are right to be concerned: one paralysed young player, and there have been several around the world, is one too many.

So many serious, long-term injuries will require bigger squads and therefore greater financial outlay and commitment. Expecting any player to play much more than twenty games a season will become impossible in the future unless the physicality of the sport is reduced. And that seems unlikely.

Only by the careful management of players by the union, as has been possible in countries like New Zealand and Ireland, will players enjoy careers of longevity even approaching those of their predecessors. Without that, we are going to see players lasting only perhaps five or six years at the top level.

Already, some have voted with their feet and rejected a professional rugby career. Professionalism has forced young men of academic capabilities to choose between the game and their career. You have to say, the most sensible have gone for the career. That, too, has been to rugby's detriment.

Years of involvement in the game by future doctors, lawyers, dentists, captains of industry and financial experts brought a unique flavour to this sport. On major tours of past times such as those of the British and Irish Lions, Welsh steelworkers and miners shared rooms with Cambridge University students or brilliant scientists. This extraordinary pot-pourri of human intellect and character defined the game. Alas, in its professional guise, there has been a levelling out and rugby union has been the poorer for the loss.

Only the naïve would suggest that rugby should never have gone professional. It had to, there was no alternative. Commercial elements outside the game would have seen to that and in their hands, no protection whatever would have been afforded the old ways and customs of the sport.

But that said, it was surely disappointing that the leaders of the game abrogated so utterly their responsibilities by simply allowing a free-for-all. No business could expect salvation in its field for so crass a policy, so poorly prepared a strategy. And never forget, the moment rugby union became professional it was first and foremost a business. This great game that has meant so much to so many the world over these last 100 years and more was surely entitled to expect something better from those with its control in their hands. The old gentlemen of the International Rugby Board merit most of the condemnation

Previous pages: Preparing for impact. New Zealand's Jerry Collins is about to hammer into England's Jonny Wilkinson in the 2003 Test at Westpac Stadium, Wellington. England won 15-13.

that has been directed their way in recent years since their panic decision.

But that is not to say a better future cannot be spied. Clearly, it can. Rugby union remains a hugely popular game throughout the world, as evidenced by the rise of its flagship event, the Rugby World Cup, to a position of third top sports event in the world, behind only the FIFA Football World Cup and the Olympics. That is some achievement for a sport that barely a dozen years ago was still losing so many of its best players to rugby league. But to achieve its complete potential in the future, the sport will need greater wisdom.

It is surely not beyond the capacity of a game that has produced so many outstanding human beings down the years to find leaders of acumen and character, people able to chart a successful path for the future.

On the field, the emphasis now surely needs to turn for the first time since professionalism arrived to the intricacies of attack. At its best, at its lively, most inventive and creative best, this game still has few equals. But the defence-riddled game that has quickly emerged these last twelve years, spawned by professionalism, has damaged that wonderful side of the sport. A significant re-think is now surely long overdue, and at the start of 2007 there were clear signs that process was being instigated and led by New Zealand.

The formidable All Blacks had retained all the elements of their traditional forward power but, unlike so many countries in the modern era, they had retained a culture of enterprise, pace and decision-making behind the scrum that was a throwback to days of yore. All credit and commendation to them under the shrewd tutelage of their coach, Graham Henry, and his knowledgeable assistants, Steve Hansen and Wayne Smith.

If New Zealand wins the 2007 Rugby World Cup with this compelling brand of power, pace and adventure, the three forged on an attacking creed, then rugby union could have no finer role model with which to go forward in the coming years. The last two World Cups, won by Australia in 1999 and England in 2003, were achieved with a heavy accent on defensive security. Clearly, defence is important but what the game plainly needs now is an example of the attacking philosophy at its best, good enough to win a World Cup.

And yet, some believe things may not be as they appear. Australian coach John Connolly admits there has probably been too much focus on defence in the first decade of professionalism. But, as he says, 'We have an inherent challenge in rugby. There are fifteen players on each side strung out across a 70-metre wide field. That means you have someone standing just over every 4 metres. That being the case, the balance is inevitably on the side of defence and once professionalism arrived, it was always going to mean that professional rugby teams would become much more organized. Professionalism offered the time to perfect that organization. Yet having made that point, you still see many matches where 40 or more points are scored. Most games used to be far less than that in the old days of amateurism. You even had matches ending up 6-3 or 9-8! So that tells you the game may be freer than we think it is.'

Perhaps alterations to the laws, as urged by that great Frenchman Jean-Pierre Rives elsewhere in this book, can help transfer the focus from defence to attack. The IRB, assisted by their excellent refereeing administrator Paddy O'Brien (another New Zealander who talks immense sense) spent most of 2006 studying proposals for major law changes. If implemented, they could take effect early in 2008 and help transform the focus of players and coaches alike.

But on another theme, unless urgent and remedial action is taken, future World Cups may well come down to a meaningful contest between only a handful of nations. Professionalism has widened the gap between the traditionally strong rugby-playing nations and the so-called lesser countries.

These smaller nations, one hastens to add, are in no way inferior in their love and enthusiasm for the game. Indeed, some suggest they now hold the candle of what was pure rugby union as a game. The tide of commercialism has yet to engulf them; indeed, some would hope it never does.

Yet without it, how can they hope even to keep up with nations where money now fuels the entire professional game, still less match them at some undefined future point in time? The 2007 Rugby World Cup will doubtless see a repeat of some of the absurd score lines of past tournaments: the 142-0 annihilation of Namibia by Australia in the 2003 tournament, New Zealand's 101-3 flogging of Italy in the 1999 competition and their 145-17 slaughter of Japan in the 1995 World Cup. These mismatches reveal only one thing: rugby union is not in truth a sport of worldwide strength. It may boast more than 100 member nations, but only a tiny percentage are serious players on the world stage. This imbalance needs to be addressed if the sport is genuinely to go forward.

Lote Tuqiri in action during Australia's 142-0 victory over Namibia in the Rugby World Cup Pool A match at the Oval Stadium, Adelaide in 2003.

Commendably, the IRB is investing some significant sums of money into most of the financially impoverished countries in a bid to raise playing levels. But greater innovation might well be required to have a profound effect. For example, why shouldn't a certain number of former internationals from countries like France and England move if they wish to somewhere like Italy and, after a year or eighteen months residential qualification, become available for that country? It would raise not just playing standards but the entire profile of the game.

In a sport like professional soccer where no team of world power, not even the likes of Brazil, Argentina, Germany, France or Italy can be sure of reaching the last four of a World Cup, it is a different story. Playing numbers the world over ensure football's long-held position of ascendancy will remain.

Rugby is different, an altogether smaller game that badly needs strengthening around the globe in so many countries. Relaxing the rules of qualification may be one answer to what seems a long-term problem.

The danger is that the gap that currently exists will become a chasm. Today, in 2007, countries once regarded as leading rugby nations like Scotland are struggling to match the pace of progression being set by the likes of New Zealand. In truth, barely three countries are likely to challenge New Zealand's envisaged superiority at the 2007 Rugby World Cup: perhaps Australia and South Africa, maybe France. Ireland has improved significantly but may be too reliant on just a few key individuals, in stark contrast to the rich pool of playing talent currently enjoyed by New Zealand.

As for England, the defending champions, they sank as low as seventh in the IRB world rankings by the end of 2006, diminished by a combination of bitter in-fighting, poor leadership at the top of their union and a lack of quality players to replace the excellence of their 2003 men: Martin Johnson, Lawrence Dallaglio, Richard Hill, Jonny Wilkinson, Neil Back, Will Greenwood.

It will be to the game's ruling body, the IRB, that the sport will look increasingly for leadership, guidance, wisdom and vision. Can it provide such qualities whilst at the same time holding the sport together for universal benefit? It will not be an easy task.

It is always better to consider the glass half full, rather than half empty. Perhaps then it is worth reiterating the viewpoint that this game has produced so many people of outstanding qualities that in its hour of need it will find such minds to take it forward to greater prosperity, not just for the already rich and powerful, but for all nations that embrace the sport.

Rugby's history is littered with great deeds, acts of bravery, courage and glory by men of supreme talent, character and no small intellect. There seems no reason why it should not enjoy similarly propitious times in the future. But calm, cool heads filled with wisdom will be required to guide it towards those sunny climes, not just at the professional levels of the sport but lower down, too, if so much of what rugby always meant is to be retained for the benefit of future generations, whatever their playing standards.

Opposite: The French team warms up at the atmospheric Stade de France, venue of the 2007 World Cup Final.

Records

British & Irish Lions Tours

1950: Australia and New Zealand

(First Post–War Lions Tour)

Lions	9–9	New Zealand	Dunedin
Lions	0–8	New Zealand	Christchurch
Lions	3–6	New Zealand	Wellington
Lions	8–11	New Zealand	Auckland
Lions	19–6	Australia	Brisbane
Lions	24–3	Australia	Sydney

1955: South Africa

Lions	23–22	South Africa	Johannesburg
Lions	9–25	South Africa	Cape Town
Lions	9–6	South Africa	Pretoria
Lions	8–22	South Africa	Port Elizabeth

1959: Australia and New Zealand

Lions	17–6	Australia	Brisbane
Lions	24–3	Australia	Sydney
Lions	17–18	New Zealand	Dunedin
Lions	8–11	New Zealand	Wellington
Lions	8–22	New Zealand	Christchurch
Lions	9–6	New Zealand	Auckland

1962: South Africa

Lions	3–3	South Africa	Johannesburg
Lions	0–3	South Africa	Durban
Lions	3–8	South Africa	Cape Town
Lions	14–34	South Africa	Bloemfonein

1966: Australia, New Zealand and Canada

Lions	11–8	Australia	Sydney
Lions	31–0	Australia	Brisbane
Lions	3–20	New Zealand	Dunedin
Lions	12–16	New Zealand	Wellington
Lions	6–19	New Zealand	Christchurch
Lions	11–24	New Zealand	Auckland
Lions	19–8	Canada	Toronto

1968: South Africa

Lions	20–25	South Africa	Pretoria
Lions	6–6	South Africa	Port Elizabeth
Lions	6–11	South Africa	Cape Town
Lions	6–19	South Africa	Johannesburg

1971: New Zealand

Lions	9–3	New Zealand	Dunedin
Lions	12–22	New Zealand	Christchurch
Lions	13–3	New Zealand	Wellington
Lions	14–14	New Zealand	Auckland

1974: South Africa

Lions	12–3	South Africa	Cape Town
Lions	28–9	South Africa	Pretoria
Lions	26–9	South Africa	Port Elizabeth
Lions	13–13	South Africa	Johannesburg

1977: New Zealand

Lions	12–16	New Zealand	Wellington
Lions	13–9	New Zealand	Christchurch
Lions	7–19	New Zealand	Dunedin
Lions	9–10	New Zealand	Auckland

1980: South Africa

Lions	22–26	South Africa	Cape Town
Lions	19–26	South Africa	Bloemfontein
Lions	10–12	South Africa	Port Elizabeth
Lions	17–13	South Africa	Pretoria

1983: New Zealand

Lions	12–16	New Zealand	Christchurch
Lions	0–9	New Zealand	Wellington
Lions	8–15	New Zealand	Dunedin
Lions	6–38	New Zealand	Auckland

1989: Australia
Lions	12–30	Australia	Sydney
Lions	19–12	Australia	Brisbane
Lions	19–18	Australia	Sydney
Lions	19–15	Anzac XV	Brisbane

1993: New Zealand
Lions	18–20	New Zealand	Christchurch
Lions	20–7	New Zealand	Wellington
Lions	13–30	New Zealand	Auckland

1997: South Africa
Lions	25–16	South Africa	Cape Town
Lions	18–15	South Africa	Durban
Lions	16–35	South Africa	Johannesburg

2001: Australia
Lions	29–13	Australia	Brisbane
Lions	14–35	Australia	Melbourne
Lions	23–29	Australia	Sydney

2005: Argentina and New Zealand
Lions	25–25	Argentina	Cardiff
Lions	3–21	New Zealand	Christchurch
Lions	18–48	New Zealand	Wellington
Lions	19–38	New Zealand	Auckland

Five & Six Nations Championships

Year	Winner	Notes
1947	Wales & England	France re-join after WWII
1948	Ireland	Grand Slam Winners
1949	Ireland	Triple Crown Winners
1950	Wales	Grand Slam Winners
1951	Ireland	
1952	Wales	Grand Slam Winners
1953	England	
1954	England, France & Wales	England win Triple Crown
1955	France & Wales	
1956	Wales	
1957	England	Grand Slam Winners
1958	England	
1959	France	
1960	France & England	England win Triple Crown
1961	France	
1962	France	
1963	England	
1964	Scotland & Wales	
1965	Wales	
1966	Wales	
1967	France	
1968	France	Grand Slam Winners
1969	Wales	Triple Crown Winners
1970	France & Wales	
1971	Wales	Grand Slam Winners
1972	TOURNAMENT NOT COMPLETED	
1973	Five-way tie	
1974	Ireland	
1975	Wales	Triple Crown Winners
1976	Wales	Grand Slam Winners
1977	France	Grand Slam Winners, Wales win Triple Crown
1978	Wales	Grand Slam Winners
1979	Wales	Triple Crown Winner
1980	England	Grand Slam Winners
1981	France	Grand Slam Winners
1982	Ireland	Triple Crown Winners
1983	France & Ireland	
1984	Scotland	Grand Slam Winners
1985	Ireland	Triple Crown Winners
1986	France & Scotland	
1987	France	Grand Slam Winners
1988	Wales & France	Wales win Triple Crown
1989	France	
1990	Scotland	Grand Slam Winners
1991	England	Grand Slam Winners
1992	England	Grand Slam Winners
1993	France	
1994	Wales	
1995	England	Grand Slam Winners
1996	England	Triple Crown winners
1997	France	Grand Slam Winners, England win Triple Crown
1998	France	Grand Slam Winners, England win Triple Crown
1999	Scotland	

(Competition becomes Six Nations)

Year	Winner	Notes
2000	England	Italy joins
2001	England	
2002	France	Grand Slam Winners, England win Triple Crown
2003	England	Grand Slam Winners
2004	France	Grand Slam Winners, Ireland win Triple Crown
2005	Wales	Grand Slam Winners
2006	France	Ireland win Triple Crown
2007	France	Ireland win Triple Crown

Rugby World Cup – William Webb Ellis Trophy

1987: NEW ZEALAND AND AUSTRALIA
FIRST RUGBY WORLD CUP
Quarter Finals

New Zealand	30–3	Scotland	Christchurch
France	31–16	Fiji	Auckland
Australia	33–15	Ireland	Sydney
Wales	16–3	England	Brisbane

Semi Finals

France	30–24	Australia	Sydney
New Zealand	49–6	Wales	Brisbane

Final

NEW ZEALAND	29–9	France	Auckland

1991: ENGLAND, FRANCE, IRELAND, SCOTLAND, WALES
Quarter Finals

Scotland	28–6	W. Samoa	Edinburgh
England	19–10	France	Paris
Australia	19–18	Ireland	Dublin
New Zealand	29–13	Canada	Lille

Semi Finals

England	9–6	Scotland	Edinburgh
Australia	16–6	New Zealand	Dublin

Final

AUSTRALIA	12–6	England	Twickenham

1995: SOUTH AFRICA
Quarter Finals

France	36–12	Ireland	Durban
South Africa	42–14	W. Samoa	Johannesburg
England	25–22	Australia	Cape Town
New Zealand	48–30	Scotland	Pretoria

Semi Finals

South Africa	19–15	France	Durban
New Zealand	45–29	England	Cape Town

Final

SOUTH AFRICA	15–12	New Zealand	Johannesburg
	(after extra time)		

1999: WALES, ENGLAND, FRANCE, SCOTLAND, IRELAND
Quarter Finals

Australia	24–9	Wales	Cardiff
South Africa	44–21	England	Paris
New Zealand	30–18	Scotland	Edinburgh
France	47–26	Argentina	Dublin

Semi Finals

Australia	27–21	South Africa	Twickenham
France	43–31	New Zealand	Twickenham

Final

AUSTRALIA	35–12	France	Cardiff

2003: AUSTRALIA
Quarter Finals

New Zealand	29–9	South Africa	Melbourne
Australia	33–16	Scotland	Brisbane
France	43–21	Ireland	Melbourne
England	28–17	Wales	Brisbane

Semi Finals

Australia	22–10	New Zealand	Sydney
England	24–7	France	Sydney

Final

ENGLAND	20–17	Australia	Sydney
	(after extra time)		

Tri-Nations Series

1996	P	W	D	L	BP	Pts
New Zealand	4	4	0	0	1	17
South Africa	4	1	0	3	2	6
Australia	4	1	0	3	2	6

New Zealand	43–6	Australia	Wellington
Australia	21–16	South Africa	Sydney
New Zealand	15–11	South Africa	Christchurch
Australia	25–35	New Zealand	Brisbane
South Africa	25–19	Australia	Bloemfontein
South Africa	18–29	New Zealand	Cape Town

1997	P	W	D	L	BP	Pts
New Zealand	4	4	0	0	2	18
South Africa	4	1	0	3	3	7
Australia	4	1	0	3	2	6

South Africa	32–35	New Zealand	Johannesburg
Australia	18–33	New Zealand	Melbourne
Australia	32–20	South Africa	Brisbane
New Zealand	55–35	South Africa	Auckland
New Zealand	36–24	Australia	Dunedin
South Africa	61–22	Australia	Pretoria

1998	P	W	D	L	BP	Pts
South Africa	4	4	0	0	1	17
Australia	4	2	0	2	2	10
New Zealand	4	0	0	4	2	2

Australia	24–16	New Zealand	Melbourne
Australia	13–14	South Africa	Perth
New Zealand	3–13	South Africa	Wellington
New Zealand	23–27	Australia	Christchurch
South Africa	24–23	New Zealand	Durban
South Africa	29–15	Australia	Pretoria

1999	P	W	D	L	BP	Pts
New Zealand	4	3	0	1	0	12
Australia	4	2	0	2	2	10
South Africa	4	1	0	3	0	4

New Zealand	28–0	South Africa	Dunedin
Australia	32–6	South Africa	Brisbane
New Zealand	34–15	Australia	Auckland
South Africa	18–34	New Zealand	Pretoria
South Africa	10–9	Australia	Johannesburg
Australia	28–7	New Zealand	Sydney

2000	P	W	D	L	BP	Pts
Australia	4	3	0	1	2	14
New Zealand	4	2	0	2	4	12
South Africa	4	1	0	3	2	6

Australia	35–39	New Zealand	Sydney
New Zealand	25–12	South Africa	Christchurch
Australia	26–6	South Africa	Sydney
New Zealand	23–24	Australia	Wellington
South Africa	46–40	New Zealand	Johannesburg
South Africa	18–19	Australia	Durban

2001	P	W	D	L	BP	Pts
Australia	4	2	1	1	1	11
New Zealand	4	2	0	2	1	9
South Africa	4	1	1	2	2	6

South Africa	3–12	New Zealand	Cape Town
South Africa	20–15	Australia	Pretoria
New Zealand	15–23	Australia	Dunedin
Australia	14–14	South Africa	Perth
New Zealand	26–15	South Africa	Auckland
Australia	29–26	New Zealand	Sydney

2002	P	W	D	L	BP	Pts
New Zealand	**4**	**3**	**0**	**1**	**3**	**15**
Australia	4	2	0	1	3	11
South Africa	4	1	0	3	3	7

New Zealand	12–6	Australia	Christchurch
New Zealand	41–20	South Africa	Wellington
Australia	38–27	South Africa	Brisbane
Australia	16–14	New Zealand	Sydney
South Africa	23–30	New Zealand	Durban
South Africa	33–31	Australia	Johannesburg

2003	P	W	D	L	BP	Pts
New Zealand	**4**	**4**	**0**	**0**	**2**	**18**
Australia	4	1	0	3	2	6
South Africa	4	1	0	3	0	2

South Africa	26–22	Australia	Cape Town
South Africa	16–52	New Zealand	Pretoria
Australia	21–50	New Zealand	Sydney
Australia	29–9	South Africa	Brisbane
New Zealand	19–11	South Africa	Dunedin
New Zealand	21–17	Australia	Auckland

2004	P	W	D	L	BP	Pts
South Africa	**4**	**2**	**0**	**2**	**3**	**11**
Australia	4	2	0	2	2	10
New Zealand	4	2	0	2	1	9

New Zealand	16–7	Australia	Wellington
New Zealand	23–21	South Africa	Christchurch
Australia	30–26	South Africa	Perth
Australia	23–18	New Zealand	Sydney
South Africa	40–26	New Zealand	Johannesburg
South Africa	23–19	Australia	Durban

2005	P	W	D	L	BP	Pts
New Zealand	**4**	**3**	**0**	**1**	**3**	**15**
South Africa	4	3	0	1	1	13
Australia	4	0	0	4	3	3

South Africa	22–16	Australia	Pretoria
South Africa	22–16	New Zealand	Cape Town
Australia	13–30	New Zealand	Sydney
Australia	19–22	South Africa	Perth
New Zealand	31–27	South Africa	Dunedin
New Zealand	34–24	Australia	Auckland

2006 NEW, EXPANDED TOURNAMENT FORMAT
Each team played one another 3 times

2006	P	W	D	L	BP	Pts
New Zealand	**6**	**5**	**0**	**1**	**3**	**23**
Australia	6	2	0	4	3	11
South Africa	6	2	0	4	1	9

South Africa	24–16	Australia	Johannesburg
South Africa	21–20	New Zealand	Rustenburg
South Africa	26–45	New Zealand	Pretoria
New Zealand	34–27	Australia	Auckland
Australia	20–18	South Africa	Sydney
Australia	9–13	New Zealand	Brisbane
New Zealand	35–17	South Africa	Wellington
Australia	49–0	South Africa	Brisbane
New Zealand	32–12	Australia	Christchurch

In 2007 the Tri-Nations will revert back to its original format.

POINTS SCHEDULE

Win = 4 points		**Bonus points:**
Draw = 2 points		1 = scoring 4 tries in game
Loss = 0 points		1 = loss by up to 7 points

ALL–TIME TRI–NATIONS TABLE

	P	W	L	D	PF	PA	PD	TD	TA	BP	PTS
NZ	46	32	14	0	1264	924	340	90	73	22	150
AUS	46	18	27	1	979	1070	-91	75	77	24	98
SA	46	18	27	1	940	1189	-249	72	87	16	90

Index

Picture Credits

The publishers would like to thank the following sources for their kind permission to reproduce the pictures in this book.